NATIVE TREE
FOR YOU

C000268667

JILL, DUCHESS OF HAMILTON

CHRISTOPHER HUMPHRIES

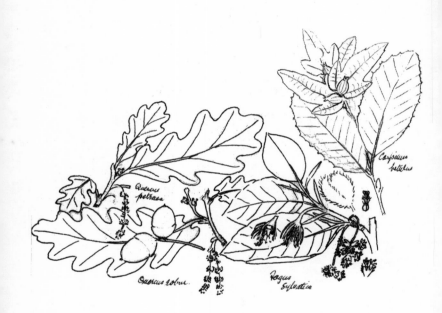

Quercus petraea

Quercus robur

Fagus sylvatica

Carpinus betulus

NATIVE TREES AND SHRUBS
FOR YOUR GARDEN

JILL, DUCHESS OF HAMILTON
CHRISTOPHER HUMPHRIES

Preface by Sue Minter, The Eden Project

And groups under the dreaming garden-trees,
And the full moon and the white evening star.
'Thyrsis', Matthew Arnold (1822–88)

FRANCES LINCOLN

**NATIVE TREES AND SHRUBS
FOR YOUR GARDEN**

Frances Lincoln Limited
4 Torriano Mews
Torriano Avenue
London NW5 2RZ

First Frances Lincoln edition: 2005

Printed in Great Britain

ISBN 0 7112 2215 0

CONTENTS

Tilia platyphyllos Scop.

Teme Valley Malvern Woods.

July. 17. 1932. parson. F. M. Day

Tribute to the Reverend
WILLIAM KEBLE MARTIN

This, the first full-length book on gardening with British native trees and shrubs, coincides with the fortieth anniversary of the Rev. William Keble Martin's *Concise Flora of the British Isles in Colour*. A bestseller in 1965, it was a landmark in nature conservation, and celebrated Keble Martin's lifetime of research and draughtsmanship. Thirty of his charming drawings, in their original form as line sketches, are published for the first time in the present book (in the 1965 book nearly 1,400 species were specially grouped and coloured for printing).

William Keble Martin was born in 1877 and educated at Marlborough, where he showed such skill at butterfly-collecting and botany that he went on to read botany at Oxford. Here he learned how to draw specimens under a microscope and study the flora of the British Isles. But instead of a career in science he was ordained, and for eighteen years he worked first as a curate and then as a vicar in the industrial parishes of northern England and, after the outbreak of World War One, as a chaplain to the forces in France. When peace came in 1918, like the poet-vicar Andrew Marvell three centuries earlier, he moved to his beloved Devon. Here he was vicar in various parishes, including Torrington, Haccombe and Dartington. An active member of botanical circles, he was elected a Fellow of the Linnean Society in 1928, and eleven years later edited a comprehensive *Flora of Devon* for the Devon Association. That year he was invited to sit on the first Nature Reserves Committee. He retired in 1949 at the age of 72, but still worked in the church, taking locums all over the country; in 1965, at the age of 89, he married for the second time. In June 1966 he received an honorary degree of Doctor of Science from Exeter University and in the following November he was asked by the Post Office to submit designs for an issue of wild flower stamps; four of these were accepted and issued in April 1967. Just before he died at the age of 92 in November 1969, he published his autobiography, *Over the Hills*. After his death, his widow Florence presented his original drawings to the Linnean Society, together with his microscope, mounted lens and a small box of watercolours and brushes.

Sketches by Keble Martin may be seen above, and on pages 2, 6, 18, 28, 32, 37, 50, 53, 61, 67, 73, 106, 108, 117, 134, 137, 153, 154, 163, 165, 172, 174, 179, 184, 188, 193, 203, 207 and 210. Those on pages 18 and 210 are reproduced at actual size.

PREFACE

It is a fact almost universally acknowledged that people all over the world undervalue and take for granted their native floras. Why this should be is perhaps not so mysterious: the native is familiar, unremarkable and without the stories of derring-do that so often accompany the introduction of exotics. In the early eighteenth century, the apothecary William Curtis found this to his cost – his beautifully illustrated flora of London and its environs, *Flora Londinensis*, was a commercial flop whereas its successor, *Curtis's Botanical Magazine*, was snapped up by a public eager to see new exotics illustrated in colour, each accompanied by a botanical description, a publication which is still issued today.

Yet when people are asked what they are homesick for when away from Britain, it is often native plants and ecosystems that they mention. 'The bluebell woods of Ruislip' and 'the beech hangers of Sarratt' would be my contribution here – and I only need to reflect that the former have largely disappeared under housing estates and the latter felled by storms to realise that these are plants under threat by population pressure and climate change. The phenomenon of people decrying their 'own' floras is common in Australia, New Zealand and South Africa, which all have particularly rich, endemic floras of their own. The flora of the UK is much less rich by comparison: botanists call it a 'depauperate post-glacial flora' – one diminished in richness of species by extinctions caused by the Ice Ages. But there is a change afoot in the appreciation of native floras, whether rich or poor ones.

This change has been engendered by the Convention on Biological Diversity, spawned by the Earth Summit in Rio de Janeiro of 1992. Floras are now seen as a matter of national pride, to be conserved and utilised for the national good in their own right, or in their genes and products obtained from them, or in knowledge about their use. This change has caused rapid revision of the remits of botanic gardens around the world. The Royal Botanic Gardens, Kew, for example, long concerned with tropical botany and particularly tropical economic botany, now has a Millennium Seed Bank to conserve Britain's biodiversity as well as that of the dry tropics; it recently ran a DEFRA-funded festival of the UK's wild plants entitled 'Go Wild'. This 'return of the native' has been scientifically informed by an understanding of DNA sequencing in defining native genotypes and an increasing understanding of the ecological basis of complex food systems in which native plants may be important keystones.

This book is aimed at the gardener. Gardeners are often appreciated in terms of their contribution to 'carbon sinks' and to the richness of wildlife in urban and suburban gardens (compared to monocropped agricultural fields). What is less appreciated is the potential of gardeners, in growing native plants, to contribute to the retention of characteristic landscapes and local distinctiveness, which may be visual, part of local cottage industry or local myth and folklore. All of this is covered here, along with some interesting examples of the cultural importance of the plants in poetry. Britain's native plants are the frame into which later exotic introductions have been fitted and, due to their long association with our developing culture, they often have some of the most interesting stories attached to them. Just as other cultures are defending the value of their floras, we should not forget the value of our own.

SUE MINTER
Director of Horticulture
The Eden Project

WHY GROW NATIVE TREES AND SHRUBS?

He that planteth a tree is a servant of God;
He provideth a kindness for many generations
   Henry van Dyke (1852–1933)

William Shakespeare (1564–1616) never saw a rhododendron. Neither did Geoffrey Chaucer (c.1345–1400) nor John Milton (1608–74). Until the Middle Ages – with the exception of cereal crops brought in by Neolithic farmers and other plants brought in by the Romans – there were few foreign species growing in the British Isles. James 1 of Scotland (1394–1437) described the garden at Windsor Castle, where he was imprisoned for eighteen years, as 'A garden faire, and . . . a green lawn . . . and hawthorn hedges entwined . . . and amid every bough might be seen the sharp green sweet juniper' (*King's Quair*). Shakespeare mentions 180 different plants in his plays, of which over three-quarters are native species. Before the steady influx of the exotic, local plants such as hawthorn, holly, beech, oak and juniper formed the backbone of English and Scottish gardens.

The dramatic change in the British landscape began when sea captains realised that the British Isles could support an unusually wide variety of plants. The same favourable conditions – a benign maritime climate, a variety of soils and terrain – that produce a fascinatingly wide range of native flora also enable English gardens to grow a wider range of exotic plants than anywhere else in the world. Exotic plants were brought over from the Americas from the seventeenth century onwards, but the greatest impact was in the nineteenth century. The decks of ships from Africa, the Americas, China, India, the Pacific countries and countless other parts of the globe were crowded with new species, risking salt spray and waves, coming to be sold in Britain.

According to the botanist Anthony Huxley, the number of plant types introduced to Britain were: 84 in the sixteenth century, 940 in the seventeenth and 8,938 in the eighteenth. The Victorian botanical author John Claudius Loudon (1783–1843) estimated that by the beginning of the 1800s 13,140 plants were in cultivation in the British Isles, of which just 1,400 were natives. Now there are over 66,000 different species available on sale.

The British landscape boasts a great diversity of flowering plants, but natives now comprise a small number in total: just 1,785 species, of which only around a hundred different species are trees and shrubs. Between 1750 and 1830 approximately 6.8 million acres in England alone were brought into private cultivation as a result of the Enclosure Acts; before that, native trees and shrubs played a large part in ancient, natural and semi-natural forests. Now, however, the role of native trees is a lower priority. In England, the 2001 Inventory of Woodlands and Trees estimated that woodland was approximately 8.4 per cent of the total land cover, with only a small percentage comprising native trees. In Scotland 17 per cent of the land is covered with trees, but mostly introduced species. Until the introduction of sheep-farming and the woollen industry that coincided with the bleak period after Culloden, the hills of Scotland were quite heavily forested.

Alarmed at the decrease in native trees, DEFRA (Department of Environment, Farming and Rural Affairs) has schemes to supply free native trees to farmers and councils. Apart from being hardy and requiring minimal maintenance, native trees and shrubs are attractive alternatives to exotics. But less than 3 per cent of native plants are used by landscape architects, and they comprise only a small percentage of those sold commercially in Britain.

However, the growing of native plants is enjoying a revival. Many gardeners now want to embrace practices that are more sustainable and less damaging to the environment, and interest is increasing in the folklore, geography and literature of native plants. Other gardeners are redressing the loss of habitat that has turned gardens into refuges for wildlife. Indigenous plants are uniquely adapted to local climate, soil and wildlife; they are easy to grow, low in maintenance, do not need chemicals and can withstand long periods of dryness. Jane Nicolas, one of the new wave of landscape gardeners who uses native plants, claims: 'They work better – they know why they are there. They are not being forced to live where conditions are not ideal.' Her designs feature hawthorn, hazel, willow, yew, oak, beech, hornbeam, holly and ash.

Because most British plants are relatives of species from mainland Europe, apart from the difficulty of sourcing them, it is often hard to be sure a tree is not foreign in origin. The majority of oak or birch saplings on sale in Britain have travelled by truck over the Alps from Italy, Hungary, Romania and other southern European countries where they grow more quickly and are cheaper. Of the estimated 80 million broad-leaved shrubs and trees planted annually each year in Britain, 56 million are from the Continent (this figure does not include the 30 tonnes of Dutch acorns imported annually to grow here). Recently, however, the situation has improved because of interest in genetic 'localness': the number of 'cottage industry' small tree nurseries producing trees for local niche markets has increased, and publicity by organisations such as *Flora Locale* and the Woodland Trust has helped.

The increasing demand for British native trees and shrubs has heightened the issue of seed origin, and *Flora Locale* has raised awareness of the need for native sources and suppliers. The Forestry Commission recommend that foresters create new native woodlands by planting, where possible, trees grown from seed collected locally (Forestry Authority Practice Note FCPN8: *Using Local Stock for Planting Native Trees and Shrubs*).

WHAT DOES 'NATIVE' MEAN? The generally accepted definition of a British native or indigenous plant is one that has not been introduced by man (for example, the eucalyptus or weeping willow), and that arrived in the British Isles without human intervention before the Romans colonised Britain in 43 AD. Many native plants were present in the British Isles at the end of the last Ice Age when Britain was part of the fringe of Continental Europe and the Thames was a tributary of the Rhine. As the ice retreated the land was colonised, initially by trees such as birch and Scots pine, with the last arrivals being species such as beech, oak and hornbeam. After the seas rose at the end of the Ice Age, cutting off what are now the British Isles with the English Channel, Britain was left with a limited number of native trees, but a larger number of shrubs – all identifiable using DNA fingerprinting (which has also allowed botanists to trace relationships to the Mediterranean region).

In the 5,000 years since the complete separation of Britain from the Continent, plants have evolved in different ways. Even those that do not appear to be distinct, such as certain species of dog rose, vary minutely in chemical composition in different regions. Most of the Continent has very warm summers and very cold winters, whereas the British climate is more temperate due to the effect of the Gulf Stream and prevailing westerly or south-westerly winds. Over thousands of years the climate has affected the dates that a plant comes into leaf, or its buds burst open. In the spring, many birds rely on insects, especially caterpillars, to feed their young. If the leaves on which these insects rely are absent, the effect travels up the food chain. Hungarian hawthorn and Welsh hawthorn come into leaf at different times, as they have been conditioned to different seasons. Hungarian hawthorn in Britain unfurls its first spring leaves too late to give seasonable sustenance to the dozens of insects that rely on young hawthorn leaves, including Duke of Burgundy butterflies, yellow-tail moths and hawthorn shield-bugs. In turn, birds rely on insects to feed their young. Apart from their importance at the base of food chains, many insects are positively useful in gardens. With a variety of native plants a balance is struck, and insect damage will be relatively limited.

THE EFFECTS OF INTRODUCTIONS ON WILDLIFE

Generally, British forms of plants tend to be more resistant to frost and damp than their European counterparts, and they fruit at times more appropriate to the British animals that depend on them. There is no such thing as a universal plant that is all things to all animals. Unlike human beings who can quickly adapt to their surroundings, many native fauna have precise nutritional needs. Most animals are dependent on specific local plants; they have unique haunts and habitats and reproduce only when conditions are right. Many cannot vary their diet. Asia's panda eats only

NUMBER OF INSECT SPECIES SUPPORTED BY BRITISH NATIVE TREES

Oak (*Quercus*)	284
Willow (*Salix*)	266
Birch (*Betula*)	229
Hawthorn (*Crataegus*)	149
Blackthorn (*Prunus spinosa*)	109
Pine (*Pinus sylvestris*)	91
Alder (*Alnus*)	90
Elm (*Ulmus*)	82
Hazel (*Corylus*)	73
Beech (*Fagus*)	64
Ash (*Fraxinus*)	41
Lime (*Tilia*)	31
Hornbeam (*Carpinus*)	28

In contrast, the non-native imports sweet chestnut and rhododendron support respectively just three and one insect species. Despite its name, the London plane tree is not native to Britain, and is avoided by most birds and insects. It was imported from southern Portugal in the eighteenth century by Lord Berkeley and planted in Berkeley Square, London.

bamboo, Australia's koala relies on certain types of eucalyptus leaves and China's silkworm must have white mulberry trees. The diets of Britain's wildlife are less well-known: the barn owl requires small rodents, the caterpillar of the small tortoiseshell butterfly will eat only stinging nettles, the swift and the swallow rely on flying insects, and the goldfinch needs seeds. Without honeysuckle there would be no white admiral butterfly. Thousands of insect species rely solely on one or a few particular plants, either for nourishment or for egg-laying, and if these are absent then the insects will perish along with some of their predators. The inclusion of native plants in gardens has the benefit of assisting with food chains. Gardeners may welcome birds and butterflies, but without so-called pests there would be none of them — all butterflies were caterpillars once!

Although it is the seeds and fruits of trees that attract some birds, many others require the wide variety of insects the trees support; like frogs, dragonflies and hedgehogs, birds rely on invertebrates for protein. Although many adult birds feed partly or totally on vegetable matter, their young feed solely on insects. Slugs play an important part in disposing of waste vegetation and, in turn, are eaten by thrushes. More than 80 per cent of resident birds need small creatures, such as the caterpillars of moths, butterflies, worms and beetles, which thrive on certain native plants and live in holes in walls and buildings or in wood piles and thick leaf litter. Beetles are a vital food for hedgehogs.

Native trees and shrubs are especially suited to the soft light of the British Isles, their colours often being understated in comparison with the harsher tones of flowers from sunnier climes. The gentle beauty of Britain's flora — hedgerows fragrant with honeysuckle, white and pink wild roses — stands in contrast to the spectacular displays of imported plants. British trees and shrubs, especially hawthorn, elder and wild cherry, have lavish blossom but small flowers and mostly smallish leaves. Enticing displays can be achieved with a succession of plants coming into leaf, flower and fruit throughout the year. The dark purple sloes of blackthorn (*Prunus spinosa*) make it a splendid species for exposed gardens — and the lustrous evergreens, such as holly (*Ilex aquifolium*) and ivy

(*Hedera helix*) supply welcome berries for birds through the winter and bring cheer to the garden, explaining the use of holly for centuries as Christmas decoration.

Trees and shrubs are the framework of a garden, defining its shape, its overall appearance, forming living screens against prying eyes and even, to some extent, cutting out traffic noise and pollution from roads. They also give structure and height, shade and shelter from winds and, to a degree, dictate the growing conditions for other plants. Many new homeowners avoid planting trees, fearing that they will be slow-growing. But even quite a young tree makes an impact in a garden, and some, such as native willows and birches, grow rapidly. Shrubs disguise the bareness of a new garden, they hide fences, separate areas, soften the lines of a house, and provide flowers and scent. Climbers often grow in spaces that would not support a tree or shrub – their natural habit is to grow quickly so they can reach the light.

NOTE It is always a good idea to have a variety of different species of all plants, to guard against the effects of disease.

Salix triandra

Shirwell N. Devon

April 1903

per Miss Cadell

SIXTY-FIVE TREE PROFILES

90	*Helianthemum nummularium*	Cistaceae	ROCKROSE
92	*Hippophae rhamnoides*	Elaeagnaceae	SEA BUCKTHORN
94	*Humulus lupulus*	Cannabaceae	HOP
97	*Hypericum androsaemum*	Hypericaceae	TUTSAN
99	*Hypericum perforatum*	Hypericaceae	PERFORATE ST JOHN'S WORT
101	*Ilex aquifolium*	Aquifoliaceae	HOLLY
105	*Juniperus communis*	Cupressaceae	JUNIPER
108	*Lavatera arborea*	Malvaceae	TREE MALLOW
110	*Ligustrum vulgare*	Oleaceae	PRIVET
111	*Lonicera periclymenum*	Caprifoliaceae	HONEYSUCKLE, WOODBINE
116	*Malus sylvestris*	Rosaceae	CRAB APPLE
119	*Myrica gale*	Myricaceae	BOG MYRTLE, SWEET GALE
121	*Pinus sylvestris*	Pinaceae	SCOTS PINE
125	*Populus nigra*	Salicaceae	BLACK POPLAR
128	*Populus tremula*	Salicaceae	ASPEN
131	*Potentilla fruticosa*	Rosaceae	SHRUBBY CINQUEFOIL
133	*Prunus avium*	Rosaceae	WILD CHERRY, GEAN
136	*Prunus padus*	Rosacea	BIRD CHERRY
138	*Prunus spinosa*	Rosaceae	BLACKTHORN, SLOE
141	*Quercus robur*	Fagaceae	PEDUNCULATE OAK
147	*Rhamnus cathartica*	Rhamnaceae	BUCKTHORN, COMMON BUCKTHORN, PURGING BUCKTHORN
149	*Ribes nigrum*	Grossulariaceae	BLACKCURRANT
152	*Rosa arvensis*	Rosaceae	FIELD ROSE
154	*Rosa canina*	Rosaceae	DOG-ROSE
156	*Rosa pimpinellifolia*	Rosaceae	BURNET ROSE
159	*Rubus fruticosus*	Rosaceae	BLACKBERRY, BRAMBLE
162	*Ruscus aculeatus*	Liliaceae	BUTCHER'S BROOM

164	*Salix alba*	Salicaceae	WHITE WILLOW
167	*Salix caprea*	Salicaceae	GOAT WILLOW, PUSSY WILLOW, GREAT SALLOW
170	*Salix cinerea*	Salicaceae	GREY WILLOW GREY SALLOW
173	*Sambucus nigra*	Caprifoliaceae	ELDER
176	*Solanum dulcamara*	Solanaceae	WOODY NIGHTSHADE, BITTERSWEET
178	*Sorbus aria*	Rosaceae	COMMON WHITEBEAM
180	*Sorbus aucuparia*	Rosaceae	ROWAN, MOUNTAIN ASH
183	*Sorbus torminalis*	Rosaceae	WILD SERVICE-TREE
186	*Taxus baccata*	Taxaceae	YEW
190	*Tilia cordata*	Tiliaceae	SMALL-LEAVED LIME
193	*Ulex europaeus*	Fabaceae	GORSE, FURZE, WHIN
196	*Ulmus glabra*	Ulmaceae	MOUNTAIN ELM, WYCH ELM
199	*Ulmus procera*	Ulmaceae	ELM
202	*Vaccinium myrtillus*	Ericaceae	BILBERRY, BLAEBERRY
205	*Viburnum lantana*	Caprifoliaceae	WAYFARING-TREE
207	*Viburnum opulus*	Caprifoliaceae	GUELDER ROSE

NOTE AND ACKNOWLEDGEMENTS

The following pages have been built on the ten years of research into British native plants and also plant–animal relationships by the charity Flora for Fauna; Don Berwick; the late Penny Hart and Franklyn Perring; the late Dame Miriam Rothschild; Mike Sadka (Natural History Museum); Peter Scott (gardener to Dame Miriam Rothschild); John Simmons, and the many people who have helped us build the Postcode Plants Database (www.nhm.ac.uk/nature-online/life/plants-fungi/postcode-plants).

Thanks also to Rob Adkinson (RSPCA); Jane Baile (Predendal Manor); Mavis Batey (former president, Garden History Society); Trevor Clifford; Gina Douglas (Linnean Society); David Knott (curator, Dawyck, part of the Royal Botanic Gardens, Edinburgh); the Linnean Society; Jane Lushington (gardener, Chelsea Arts Club); the Natural History Museum; Stephen McAndrews of Hammersmith and Fulham Borough Council, and the Royal Botanic Gardens, Kew. We are also grateful to the Tree Register of the British Isles (www.tree-register.org) for information about Britain's big trees.

As the folklore and herbal medicine connected with Britain's native plants is covered in a wide range of publications, including David Allen and Gabrielle Hatfield, *Medicinal Plants in Folk Tradition: An Ethnobotany of Britain and Ireland* (Timber Press, 2004) these details have been omitted from entries. However, as the majority of early botanists were also apothecaries, if a plant was significant pharmaceutically this fact is briefly mentioned.

JILL, DUCHESS OF HAMILTON
CHRISTOPHER HUMPHRIES

Acer campestre (Aceraceae)

FIELD MAPLE

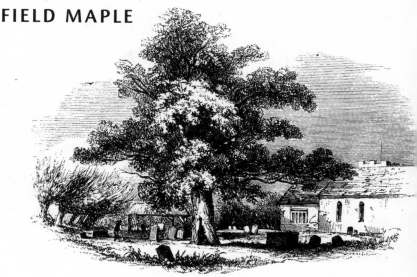

For who would rob a hermit of his weeds,
His few books, as his beads, or maple dish,
Or do his grey hairs any violence?
   'Comus', John Milton (1608–74)

With its round-headed silhouette and interesting bark, field maple is compact enough to be grown in an average suburban garden. Fast-growing, exposure-tolerant and boasting the brightest autumn foliage of any English tree, it makes an ideal feature tree. As it withstands heavy trimming, it can also be grown as part of a hedge. Just how valued it once was in gardens can be found in the writings of William Gilpin, leader of the eighteenth-century cult of the picturesque. In his landmark book, *Forest Scenery,* he wrote, 'The Maple is an uncommon Tree, though a common bush. Its wood is of little value, and it is, therefore, rarely suffered to increase. We seldom see it employed in any nobler service than in filling up its part in a hedge . . .' Maple had such a place in his heart that he was buried under one in Boldre Churchyard, New Forest, when he died in 1804.

In spring maple is decorated with clusters of small, upright, greenish-yellow flowers which appear before the leaves, while in autumn it is almost unrivalled for its golden colours. If conditions are right, the leaves turn a wonderful golden-yellow to amber before they drop. Autumn colour is dependent on cold temperatures and enough rainfall throughout the growing season to increase the sugar in the leaf, which dictates the colour change. Maple grows in a variety of soils, but prefers those that are moist, well-drained and neutral to acid. It needs a sheltered position, away from strong winds.

Most maples grown in Britain today are not native, and field maple is often confused with various cultivars introduced from America, China and Japan, or with the smaller-leafed sycamore, introduced from mainland Europe.

GROWTH Although field maple grows fairly quickly at first, it slows down once it is established and can take fifty years to reach maturity. It is capable of reaching around 25m/80ft, but seldom attains much above 10.8–15m/36–50ft.

PROPAGATION On windy days in mid-autumn, two rather flat winged seeds loosen from each fruit and are carried away from the parent tree. Those that drop in appropriate places – including hollows, hedgerows, pastures and waste lands on chalk and limestone hills – germinate slowly after lying dormant for eighteen months. Seed should be gathered in autumn and sown as soon as possible in nursery rows (germination chances decrease if seeds are kept in storage). After two to three years, transplant seedlings to their permanent sites between October and March. As maple is not easy to root from hardwood cuttings, many gardeners dig up the saplings that spontaneously spring up near mature trees.

ROLE IN LANDSCAPE Occasionally maple is seen as a tree in mixed woodland, but in the wild it is usually only a shrub in hedgerows or rural hedges. Its natural range extends only as far north as Staffordshire, Derbyshire and Durham; in Scotland and Ireland it has to be planted. It is confined mostly to lime-rich soils and chalk in Wales, and to the south and east of Britain, particularly the chalk downs of the south-east. The tallest field maple in Britain, at Sundridge Park Golf Course in Kent, is a surprising 18m/60ft high with a trunk 62cm/24in in diameter.

TRUNK, BARK AND BRANCHES When young, the trunk is a smooth, pale grey-brown or dark brown, but with age the bark is corky and becomes fissured.

LEAVES The extremely pretty leaves are opposite and simple, 5–15cm/ 2–6in long, with three to five blunt, irregular, rounded lobes, downy beneath, at least on the veins, producing a milky substance when cut.

BUDS, FLOWERS AND FRUIT Male and female flowers are found on the same tree, and appear in April and May in upright, pale, greenish-yellow clusters, each with five petals, but by the time they turn into fruit all trace of the male flowers has disappeared. The distinctive fruit consists of two sections, known as 'keys', each comprising a seed-vessel or nut, with a thin membranous extension or horizontal wing often tinged with pink.

PLANT–ANIMAL RELATIONSHIPS Abundant nectar in the flowers attracts small insects, especially bees, which effect cross-pollination and ensure the tree's survival. A delicate honeydew, sometimes found on the leaves, is relished by hairstreak butterflies as an alternative to nectar. Maple foliage is the food plant of the caterpillars of various moths, including the maple prominent, the sycamore, the buff tip, the winter, the vapourer and others. Most moths are protected from predators during the day by being heavily camouflaged with colours and patterns similar to the tree on which they usually rest. Leaf-eating weevils sometimes eat maple leaves, which can also be infested by gall mites or leaf miners. Curious marks, smaller than pinheads and similar to red pimples, are often found on the surface of the leaves – these are insect nests.

HISTORICAL AND OTHER USES The smooth-textured, creamy-brown wood is hard and superbly marked, and has been used to make furniture, bowls and other items since ancient times. Pliny extolled the fineness of its grain. Virgil, a great respecter and lover of trees, wrote of Evander: 'A maple throne, rais'd higher from the ground, Receiv'd the Trojan chief' (*The Aeneid*, Book VIII). Medieval drinking vessels, delicate bowls, spoons and platters were often made from maple, as well as mathematical and musical instruments, gun-stocks, woodwork and fretwork. In the eighteenth and nineteenth centuries the wood's curious marking, which gave it the name 'Bird's-eye Maple', was prized for inlay, picture frames and small boxes decorated with transfers, known as 'treen' objects. Vast quantities of treen boxes were manufactured and exported all over the world.

NAME Latin *acer*, maple; *campestre*, 'of the field'.

Alnus glutinosa (Betulaceae)

ALDER

The alder-trees in the first line,
They made the commencement.
Willow and quicken tree,
They were slow in their array.
  'The Battle of the Trees',
  ancient Welsh poem

Tall, narrow and pyramid-shaped, alder is a moderately sized tree or large shrub of dark colour for gardens. A traditional part of British river banks, streams and marshes, it usually grows in moist woods or pastures or by streams. With its dramatic black fissured trunk, spreading crown, egg-shaped female catkins drooping in clusters and rich green leaves, it can also be a hardy and useful tree in various types of gardens, particularly those with damp situations, streams, water-logged areas or heavy soils. Traditionally, alder is planted in water-logged conditions where its interlacing roots stabilise pond and stream banks, preventing erosion. It is particularly beneficial if planted so that it shades a pond or stream: it keeps the water cool in summer and delays freezing in winter. The area around it can be brightened with marsh marigold, yellow flag iris, sweet gale and elder. It will also grow in dry conditions provided it is kept damp for the first two to three years.

In formal gardens, it is best to shape alders when young to a single trunk and trim the branches. Alder tolerates much cutting back, allowing its height to be controlled, thus making it suitable for many places in gardens. It is quick-growing, and can be used as a nurse-tree for slower-growing trees. It is tough and wind-resistant, so is useful as a wind-break. It tolerates infertile or polluted soils, and can withstand air pollution. Handsome alders grow on Eel Brook Common, opposite the New King's Road in Fulham, London.

GROWTH HABIT Alder is not a giant of the woods. In the wild it can occasionally grow to 18m/60ft. When cultivated, in its first ten years it may reach 7.5m/25ft, but even in good conditions it rarely exceeds 15m/50ft. Although slender in appearance, the trunk eventually develops a girth of 60cm–1.8m/2–6ft. When grown for timber it is usually felled when it reaches its prime, at about fifty or sixty years old.

PROPAGATION Like birch, to which it is related, the alder seldom sets seed until it is about twenty years old. In the wild, the seeds are wind-scattered from the dangling flowers to land on female catkins. After pollination these turn into rounded cones, protecting the seed which ripens by autumn. The seeds are then shaken out of the cones, to drift on the water's surface during the winter and autumn, secreting oil that enables them to stay afloat while they are carried downstream to be deposited in damp river banks where they germinate.

One propagation method is to collect the seeds from the small cones around the last fortnight in October, and spread them in a dry place, turning them occasionally; they will be ready for sowing in April. Alder is easily raised from seed sown on any seed compost, and can be planted out from October to March. Small seedlings need bare damp earth or mud to start life – and vigorous growth relies on a root association with a bacterium that is able to fix nitrogen from the air, aiding soil fertility. Alder can also be propagated from hardwood cuttings.

ROLE IN LANDSCAPE Alder is one of the most aquatic of Britain's trees and is seldom seen far from water. Until the beginning of the twentieth century, it was found beside practically every stream and lake in much of Britain except the northern isles. Light-loving and dependent on much moisture, it grows wild in wet woods, stream borders, beside rivers and in low-lying wet fields to 500m/1,650ft. It used often to be grown in coppices and cut down for poles every nine or ten years. One of the tallest alders in Britain, 14m/49ft tall with a massive girth, is at Tretower Court, Powys, Wales.

TRUNK, BARK AND BRANCHES The bark, purplish-brown in young trees, turns brown or blackish and fissured at maturity, and is very uneven. Young shoots and twigs are sticky with mucus, and can have strange orange warts.

LEAVES The rich green leaves are 5–10cm/2–4in long, broadly ovate, stalked and usually smooth on the upper surface, with tufts of hair on the vein axils of the lower leaf surface. The doubly toothed margins are wavy and unevenly serrated, usually with a shallow notch at the tip. As with all the broad-leaved British native trees, alder is deciduous, but due to its proximity to water the leaves remain on the tree longer than with most British native trees.

BUDS, FLOWERS AND FRUIT
Between February and March, reddish flowers are borne on separate male and female catkins in clusters of two to six at the ends of branches. While the female flowers are small, up to 5mm/¼in and bud-like, the males are larger, up to 30mm/12in, and very noticeable in the form of drooping catkins which shed clouds of yellow pollen. Both male and female flowers open before the

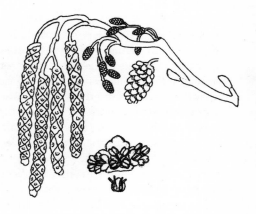

leaves are fully out, since this is the best time for wind-pollination. Once the male flowers have dispensed their pollen, they wither and fall to the ground, so that the only flowers remaining on the tree are female. Pollinated female flowers develop into woody false 'cones' of 8–28mm/3–11in, sometimes called 'berries', usually about three to six on each stalk, green at first but later black. The seed – a minute, flat nutlet, sometimes edged with a thin membranous wing – is shed from the cones in the autumn; the cones themselves can persist for several years.

PLANT–ANIMAL RELATIONSHIPS Female otters sometimes raise their cubs in 'holts' under alder roots on rivers. Alder roots bind banks, provide cover for fish and other animals, and are an important part of aquatic ecosystems. The alder is host to over ninety species of insect, including three kinds of gall-mite, and is heavily used by aquatic flies (stoneflies, caddis flies, etc.). Young alder leaves are a food plant for green hairstreak butterflies, and holly blues may lay their eggs on it if no holly is available. The leaves are also used by the caterpillars of many moths – including the lime hawk, northern winter, purple thorn, small fan-foot, small yellow wave and coronet. The flowers' strong scent attracts a host of insects, including the beetles of the scarab family which gather on the starry white flowers and feed on the pollen. When the female flowers are transformed into berries, they become winter food for a different variety of wildlife, especially birds, such as siskins and goldfinches, which in turn spread the seeds. As with many other plant seeds, they are unaffected by digestive juices and can still germinate after passing through a bird's gut.

HISTORICAL AND OTHER USES Resisting decay indefinitely under water, the alder's major use was, and often still is, in pylons, piles for jetties, pumps, troughs and sluices. Alder piles support the Rialto Bridge in Venice, and many structures in places such as Amsterdam where there is constant lapping of water. Virgil claimed that the first boats were made of alder. It was also used for divining rods to bring on rain. Like other rapidly growing trees, it has never been highly valued for furniture but when young it is brittle and easily worked. Examples of alder bowls, beakers and even combs have been found in pre-Roman archaeological sites (along with items made from hazel, elm, rowan and oak). It has been used for broom heads, toys, bobbins and small tool handles, small boxes and instrument cases. Mrs Grieve, *A Modern Herbal* (1931), wrote: 'in the Highlands of Scotland it is used for making handsome chairs, and is known as Scottish mahogany . . . The roots and knots furnish good material for cabinet-makers, and for the clogs of Lancashire mill-towns and the south of Scotland the demand exceeds the supply, and birch has to be used instead. It is also used for cart and spinning wheels, bowls, spoons, wooden heels, herring-barrel staves, etc. On the Continent it is largely used for cigar-boxes – its reddish, cedar-like wood "humidifies" the tobacco. After lying in bogs the wood has the colour but not the hardness of ebony. The branches make good charcoal, which is valuable for making gunpowder.' A tawny red dye was extracted from the bark which, as it contains a great deal of tannin, was used extensively in leather tanning. A green dye was extracted from both the female catkins and the shoots.

Whereas yew was the wood of choice for bows and arrows, with the introduction of firearms alder came to the fore (along with white willow, lime and maple). Its charcoal was rated among the best in the making of gunpowder (a mixture of sulphur, saltpetre and charcoal). Charcoal quality depends on the amount of the binder lignin in the wood; together with starches and sugars, this dictates how the wood will char. In the nineteenth century, alder was also used in the making of artificial limbs.

NAME Latin *glutinosa*, from the stickiness of the leaves. The common name is from Old English *alor, aler,* associated with the reddish-yellow of the fresh-cut timber, or from Celtic *al,* near, and *lan,* the border of a river. The Welsh name is *gwern,* from *wern,* a low-lying pasture; the Gaelic name is *fearn.*

Arbutus unedo (Ericaceae)

STRAWBERRY TREE

The strawberry tree and the crimson thorn
And Fanny's myrtle, and William's vine,
And honey of beautiful jessamine,
Are gone from the homestead where I was born.
    'A House and a Girl', William Johnson Cory (1823–92)

Good-looking and multi-stemmed, this hardy, bushy-crowned ever-green shrub or tree produces masses of bell-shaped flowers in November and December followed by spherical bright red fruit similar in appearance to strawberries. It is an excellent garden plant, gaining an interesting, twisted appearance over time. William Robinson (1838–1935), an influential writer and gardener who was also an early campaigner for growing indigenous species in gardens, used strawberry trees either mixed with exotics or as a backdrop to introduced plants: 'This beautiful shrub, though tender in inland districts, is very precious for the seashore and mild districts, not only as an evergreen, but for the beauty of its flower and fruit. Although more Irish than British, it is the one British evergreen which has to be planted with discrimination in places where the winters are severe in inland districts.'

Strawberry trees thrive in acid or limestone soils, but dislike excessive shade or ground which is too damp. Young trees need frost protection – they can be severely injured or killed in prolonged frosts – but older plants become fairly frost-tolerant and can put up with a certain amount of neglect. There is a fine example in London near the Thames in the grounds of the Bishop's Palace, Fulham.

GROWTH HABIT Strawberry trees grow slowly and are usually seen in bush form, 1–5m/39in–16½ft in height, but they can occasionally reach 9m/30ft.

PROPAGATION Harvesting seed is best done when the fruits are fully ripe and ready to fall to the ground. Some gardeners soak them in water, making it easier to separate the seeds from the fruit flesh. Once planted, seedlings need protection until they are established. As they respond badly to any root disturbance, it is better to plant them out when young.

ROLE IN LANDSCAPE Although a Mediterranean, the strawberry tree is found as a wild native tree or shrub in a few scattered places in western Ireland, mostly where there is rocky ground in scrub and woodland, from Killarney to Lough Gill, in Kerry and County Sligo. Examples growing on chalk or limestone slopes in England and Wales have usually been planted.

TRUNK, BARK AND BRANCHES The bark is rather fibrous, peeling and scaly, and a dark greyish/reddish brown. The hairy young shoots have a reddish hue.

LEAVES The hard, shiny, oval evergreen leaves have slightly dentate margins wider at the tip than near the base.

BUDS, FLOWERS AND FRUIT Pretty, waxy, white, bell-shaped flowers, white- or pink-tinged, appear in drooping clusters in autumn and early winter, followed by strawberry-like white fruits that progress into orange and red. These ripen when the tree flowers the following year, making a dramatic contrast to the lustrous dark foliage.

PLANT–ANIMAL RELATIONSHIPS The fruit is a winter food source for forest animals, especially birds.

HISTORICAL AND OTHER USES Strawberry tree wood is still used for inlay and parquetry; it used also to be made into charcoal.

NAME Latin *arbutus*, implying that people eat one and only one of the fruit. It was mentioned by Virgil in *Eclogues*, iii, 82: 'Rain is sweet to the young corn, arbutus to the weaned kids.' Its Irish name is *caitline*.

Berberis vulgaris (Berberidaceae)

WILD BARBERRY

. . . Conserves of barberries, quinces and such,
With sirops, that easeth the sickly so much . . .
'Five Hundreth Points of Good Husbandrie', Thomas Tusser, 1573

With their arched and hanging branches and bright yellow balls of blossom among sprays of dark green holly-like leaves, these thorny deciduous hedgerow shrubs are often grown to add colour to shrubberies and hedges. They can withstand hard pruning. Wild barberry thrives on all but waterlogged soils, including those that are thin, shallow or dry. It likes plenty of light, and open sunny situations encourage a profusion of flowers and berries. Once cultivated for its edible but acid berries, wild barberry is now rare: most plants were destroyed in wheat-growing areas between 1860 and 1865 when it was discovered that they were an alternate host to the wheat fungus, black rust (*Puccinia graminea*). Just how popular barberry was before its near-extermination can be seen in the garden Joseph Paxton built beside the Crystal Palace when it was reconstructed at Sydenham after the Great Exhibition of 1851: the massive terraces were originally planted with wild barberry among statuary, vases and urns. One was noted in Jane Austen's garden at Chawton near Winchester in 1815. Today, wild barberry in Britain is rare; it is often confused with the more commonly grown introduced species native to Europe – it is a large genus with both deciduous and evergreen species. With the growth of urban sprawl, the places where wild barberry can safely be grown has increased.

GROWTH HABIT A rapid grower, it usually reaches about 2.5m/8ft, sometimes 3m/10ft.

PROPAGATION It is easily grown from seeds, which quickly germinate. It can also be propagated from hardwood cuttings or by digging up its suckers.

ROLE IN LANDSCAPE Wild barberry occasionally grows in thickets and in woods, but more usually in hedgerows.

TRUNK, BARK AND BRANCHES The branches are sharp-thorned and the spine sometimes becomes covered in coral-covered burrs.

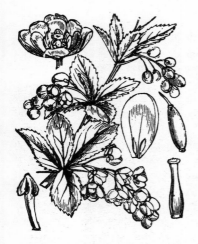

LEAVES The small- to medium-sized (2.5–6cm) pale green leaves are stiff, leathery and toothed, elliptic to obovate in shape, alternate and borne on branches in clusters.

BUDS, FLOWERS AND FRUIT Small yellow flowers, with an unpleasant smell, occur as elegant drooping pedicles in May. These give way to edible small oblong berries which are a brilliant red and hang in beautiful clusters.

PLANT–ANIMAL RELATIONSHIPS The flowers and berries provide sustenance for insects and birds, and are breeding areas for the caterpillars of the barberry carpet moth and the scarce tissue moth. Barberry bushes provide a secure nesting site for long-tailed tits and goldfinches; they have also been planted to provide cover and berries for pheasants.

HISTORICAL AND OTHER USES The astringent berries were sometimes used as a substitute for lemons in punch, or preserved in vinegar and eaten as a substitute for capers; they were valued for their medicinal properties. The root was used as a hair-dye. Barberry wood is yellow and brittle, and produces a yellow dye.

NAME Latin *berberis* from an Arabic word for fruit. In 1538, William Turner, who translated many plant names into English and devised others, called it 'Pypryge', which progressed into 'Pipperidge-bush'. The Welsh called it *eurdrain*, 'golden thorn tree'.

Betula pendula (Betulaceae)
SILVER BIRCH

Stranger! this hillock of
    misshapen stones
Is not a ruin of the ancient time,
Nor, as perchance thou rashly deem'st, the Cairn
Of some old British Chief: 'tis nothing more
Than the rude embryo of a little dome
Or pleasure-house, which was to have been built
Among the birch-trees of this rocky isle.
    'Lines written with a Slate-pencil upon a Stone',
    William Wordsworth (1770–1850)

With its slender silhouette and silvery-white bark, pendulous branches and delicate, fresh-looking foliage, silver birch is Britain's most graceful and elegant tree. Frost-hardy and able to survive urban pollution, it is valued by both town and country gardeners, especially as young trees gain height quickly. It is light-demanding, enjoying full sun or dappled shade and dry, acid, well-drained soil. As it is shallow-rooted, it needs water in extended dry periods; on poor, sandy soils its roots can become invasive. Compared to many plants, birch is trouble-free with few natural enemies and diseases, but aphid infestation can be a problem, resulting in dripping honeydew. The delicate foliage gives only dappled shade, so spring flowers can flourish beneath it. Like elder and goat willow it grows with an open habit, and is too leggy to look good in hedges. Rodney Burton, *Flora of the London Area* (1983), reported it to be increasing because of the large number of planted trees in suburban gardens which seed readily, and the lack of grazing on commons and other grassy areas.

GROWTH HABIT Although it can gain about a metre a year, birch takes about twenty years to reach its average of 15m/50ft. The tallest British example, 26m/83ft, is at Leith Hill, Surrey. Silver birch is not long-lived, usually reaching fifty years of age, eighty at the most.

PROPAGATION Propagation is entirely by seed which can be sown as soon as it ripens in autumn. The tiny winged seeds are incredibly light, weighing about 450g/1lb for 700,000 individual seeds; they are viable for only a limited time and only about 20 per cent will germinate. An easy way to collect the seed is to place small branches, broken off just before the catkins break up, in brown paper bags or sacks, and hang them upside up to dry until the seeds drop. As the seeds do not survive extended storage, some people sow them at once; others store them in moist sand until they are ready to plant the following March. The first sign of seedlings are two oval cotyledons followed by leaves; early growth is speedy. Seedlings can be transplanted between November and early March. Natural regeneration is usually excellent when protected against grazing animals.

ROLE IN LANDSCAPE Birch flourishes in a variety of situations, and grows all over the British Isles in woodland, glens, ravines, or the margins of lakes and streams, on all but the poorest and wettest soil. *Betula pendula* is the most widespread birch in Britain and, as in the rest of northern Europe, grows in woodland and on heaths. With sun and a well-drained soil, it bursts into leaf in April with flowers appearing soon afterwards, the male catkins having developed the previous autumn. Some examples, such as the Wisley Common birch in Surrey, are known for their very white stems. Struck by its lightness, silvery bark and elegance, Samuel Taylor Coleridge dubbed it the 'Lady of the Woods'. Dorothy Wordsworth described its beauty in her journal: 'Our favourite birch tree ... was yielding in a gusty wind with all its tender twigs. The sun shone upon it, and it glanced in the wind like a flying sunshiny shower.'

TRUNK, BARK AND BRANCHES Young birch has shiny reddish-brown bark and erect branches, but with age the tree develops its famous smooth, silver-white surface with thin black horizontal lines – sometimes with rough-textured, irregularly shaped patches and fissures. The slender, whippy juvenile branches are erect but, like the trunk, change with age, developing a graceful droop. In winter, the twigs appear distinctive, thin and whip-like.

LEAVES Birch begins to form glossy new leaves in mid-April. These are slender, simple, grey-green in colour and vary in shape from triangular to oval, up to 4cm/1½in long, with a sharp point at the tip and a double-toothed margin. They turn bright yellow before falling in late autumn.

BUDS, FLOWERS AND FRUIT Just as the light green, hairless leaves unfold on slender stalks in spring, the flowers appear and are grouped as catkins. Male and female catkins open on the same tree. As with most wind-pollinated plants, the flowers are without scent and devoid of bright colours. The yellow male catkins have reddish-brown scales and droop like lamb's tails; once they have shed their clouds of yellow pollen they wither and fall. In contrast, the female catkins are smaller, more erect and far less conspicuous. They are composed of overlapping green scales that protect green flowers. After fertilisation these catkins enlarge, elongate and become pendulous. After ripening, around September, they begin to break up, the scales falling away to release three tiny winged nutlets or seeds to the wind.

PLANT–ANIMAL RELATIONSHIPS Birch supports up to 230 species of insects, including the buff-tip, chevron and pale prominent moths, and the gregarious larvae of the sawfly. It is a truly hospitable tree for British wildlife. In spring and summer a wide variety of birds, especially warblers, blue tits and other insectivores, gorge themselves, while in autumn the tree plays host to a veritable avian banquet, with tits, siskins, redpolls, goldfinches and other finches feeding on the seeds, as also do small mammals, including mice and shrews. During the nesting season birch supplies the small and flexible twigs that are so vital for nest construction. Although lacking nectar, the catkins are rich in pollen which is collected by bees, the tree's most important pollinator. Its fallen leaves rot quickly to make excellent leafmould, giving cover for invertebrates. The food chain effect is well demonstrated by the caterpillars that are supported by birch: these in turn act as a food source for spiders, mites, beetles, bugs, wasps, ants, earwigs, reptiles, amphibians, birds and mammals. It also sometimes supports large colonies of aphids, which in turn attract other insects, especially ladybirds.

HISTORICAL AND OTHER USES Primitive man used cups and bowls shaped from the bark of birch (as well as other trees); some archaeologists believe that early pottery shapes were inspired by vessels previously made of vegetable material. In ancient Rome birch twigs were bunched together in *fasces* to make the lictor's rods, symbol of Roman authority, with which the way was swept for magistrates. Saunas throughout the world imitate the practice in Finland of providing clients with bunches of birch twigs with which to restore circulation, and birch rods have long been used for chastisement. Birch branches were once in common use for turned products such as bobbins, spools, brush and broom backs, pegs and toys; they are still used for brooms and brushes, especially besom brooms for gardens, for steeplechase jumps, thatching and fencing. J. C. Loudon wrote in 1842 that the 'Highlanders of Scotland make everything of it; they build their houses, make their beds and chairs, tables, dishes and spoons; construct their mills; make their carts, ploughs, harrow, gates and fences, and even manufacture [when it is dried and twisted] rope of it. The branches are employed as fuel in the distillation of whisky, the spray is used for smoking hams and herrings, for which last purpose it is preferred to every kind of wood.' Being very hard, the wood was used to make wheels and chairs. Today, birch is not used in Britain commercially for timber, because the trunks are generally not big or straight enough to be used. A weak, but quite palatable, wine used to be obtained from draining the sap in March, boiling and fermenting it.

NAME The Latin *Betula* dates back to ancient Rome; *pendula* was added later to describe the drooping shoots. The common name comes from Old English *beorc, birce*, an ancient Indo-European tree name meaning 'white' or 'shining'.

OTHER SPECIES

DOWNY BIRCH OR RED BIRCH (*Betula pubescens*)

Red birch lacks the long pendulous branches of its cousin; its young twigs are softly hairy and more upright in growth. A lovely tree, it also becomes greyish-white or silver but lacks the black diamond-shaped patches so often the feature of silver birch trunks. It is usually shorter, its catkins are narrower and leaves rounder in outline, with single rather than double teeth at the margin. Hardier and much less common than silver birch, it occurs on wetter soils, such as bogs, fens and lake margins, on acid soils up to 550m/1,800ft in the higher rainfall areas in the north and west. As it flourishes at higher altitudes, it is suited to upland or exposed gardens, moisture-retentive or in cold, exposed sites. Like the silver birch, it is host to many insects, including two species of tortricoid moths. Old trees often develop growths called 'witches' brooms' caused by a gall-forming fungus; these may be taken over by birds as nesting sites. Natural hybridisation occurs between silver and red birch, creating *Betula x aurata*.

DWARF BIRCH (*Betula nana*)

Dwarf birch, like dwarf willow (*Salix herbacea*), reaches only about 1.8m/6ft high and occurs mostly in Scotland in cold, inhospitable mountainous areas, creeping along the ground in sheltered hollows between mountains. These vanishing relics of the alpine flora of the Ice Age, together with the oyster plant (*Mertensia maritima*), the alpine lady's mantle (*Alchemilla alpina*), the Scottish primrose (*Primula scotica*) and the *Scilla verna*, are characteristic of the Scottish flora.

Buxus sempervirens (Buxaceae)

BOX

Down with the Rosemary and Bayes,
Down with the Mistleto;
In stead of Holly, now up-raise
The greener Box (for show).
The Holly hitherto did sway;
Let Box now domineere;
Until the dancing Easter-day,
Or Easter's Eve appeare.
Then youthfull Box which now hath grace,
Your houses to renew;
Grown old, surrender must his place,
Unto the crisped Yew.
　　'Ceremonies for Candlemasse Eve',
　　Robert Herrick (1591–1674)

This tough evergreen shrub with a dense green foliage of small, neat, leathery leaves has the ability to retain its shape for many years even when constantly clipped. It is seldom leggy or straggly and, together with yew, is now one of the most popular plants for hedges and topiary. Although tolerant of sun, it likes some shade during the day and keeps its shape better if clipped twice a year, in early to mid summer and in autumn. Thriving on chalk in acidic soils, it also copes with a wide range of soils as long as they are free-draining. Box has been used as a neat edging and hedge for walks and flower beds since Roman times. Pliny, author of *Naturalis Historia,* described box hedges around Roman villas. At Levens Hall in the Lake District there are examples of ambitious box topiary over three hundred years old. A more traditional use can be seen in 'The Culpeper Garden' at the restored thirteenth-century Leeds Castle in Kent, where Russell Page designed a series of clipped box hedges to create formal enclosed areas for herbs and cottage garden flowers.

Box is now so familiar as a hedge that its role as a tree is usually overlooked. At Box Hill near Dorking, Surrey, a fashionable pleasure resort in the seventeenth and eighteenth centuries (see Jane Austen's *Emma*), it still forms a grove of shade-bearing trees. Box timber was highly sought after, as can be seen in the sales records from Box Hill of 1815.

BOX · 41

GROWTH HABIT If pruned, box remains as a bush, but if left uncut it grows into a small tree. It is slow-growing. At Gunnersbury Park, London, there is an example 8m/28ft high. Straight trunks are rare; most twist in an almost snake-like manner to attain the maximum light.

PROPAGATION Seedlings spring up quite freely, but box can also be propagated by cuttings. New plants should be planted in late spring or early summer. For a border or hedge, seedlings should be spaced about 35cm/15in apart. John and Rosemary Hemphill, *The Fragrant Garden*, suggest trimming 'off firm cuttings in spring or early autumn from older established plants, dipping the pruned stems into cutting powder (optional) and putting them straight into the ground, where they remain green while making roots'. They also describe the system of burying 'three-quarters of the box in soil including leafy branches and trunk. After approximately six months, the covered parts will have established roots and can be cut off and planted.'

ROLE IN LANDSCAPE With the exception of Box Hill, the Chilterns and a few places in Hampshire on the chalk downs, box is now seldom found wild – and then only on chalk or lime-rich soils. The box that is widely planted in hedges is mostly a cultivar of one of the other thirty species of the genus, especially 'Dutch' box (*B. sempervirens suffruticosa*) which has larger leaves and grows more quickly, or 'Japanese' box (*B. microphilla*).

TRUNK, BARK AND BRANCHES The bark is slightly fissured; the branches long and drooping in its natural tree form.

LEAVES Small, more or less oblong and rounded, arranged in opposite pairs along the stem and, like most of the leaves of Britain's evergreen trees, leathery.

BUDS, FLOWERS AND FRUIT If the tree is uncut, the small, inconspicuous and insignificant yellow flowers of box appear in April and May. They lack petals and form inflorescences in the base of the leaves; these are followed by green fruits with black seeds in papery pods. The male and female flowers are separate, but in the same clusters (monoeicious).

PLANT–ANIMAL RELATIONSHIPS Like other dense-foliaged hedging plants box gives cover to birds, and is host to a small number of insects including *Psyllia buxi* which sometimes causes considerable disfigurement to a hedge. All parts of the plant are poisonous. As it contains a substance called buxine, a complex group of steroidal alkaloids, animals usually keep away from it, although poisoning has been reported in horses that eat either the plant or clippings from it.

HISTORICAL AND OTHER USES Box, along with olive, is the hardest and heaviest of all European woods, and the only one that sinks in water. Dense and even-grained, it was much valued by the Greeks who used it to make combs and musical instruments. John Gerard, London apothecary and author of *The Herball or Generall Historie of Plantes* (1597) in which many plant names first appear, wrote that the root was used by 'turners and cutlers' who called it 'dudgeon, wherewith they make dudgeon-hafted daggers'. The most important use of box by far was in wood blocks for printing, engraving and carving – the sculpture *The Virgin and Child*, cut in boxwood about 1500, can be seen in the Wallace Collection, London. Box played such an important part in the history of engraving that in 1921 the tree became the symbol for the Society of Wood Engravers. Before the invention of moveable type and printing presses, slabs made of box were turned into printing blocks – one of the finest examples was for the first printed texts of the *Roman de la Rose* of 1481. Box also had medicinal uses, the bark was an ingredient in perfume, and the leaves and sawdust were transformed into an auburn hair dye. Because of its durability, box was made into chess pieces, school rulers and various mathematical and musical instruments.

NAME Latin derived from Greek *pukos*, meaning close and dense. The word box, meaning a container, comes from early examples made of boxwood.

NOTE A new and unpleasant fungal disease, *Cylindrocladium buxicola*, is spreading in the UK. It attacks even established plants, causing leaf blight. Immediate remedial action must be taken by digging out and burning all affected plants. It particularly attacks cultivars of *B. sempervirens*, especially the dwarf 'Suffruticosa', as well as *B. microphylla* and *B. sinica*, and even the native plants at Box Hill, Surrey.

Calluna vulgaris (Ericaceae)

HEATHER

Behind the western ridge, thou glorious sun!
Shine in the slant beams of the sinking orb,
Ye purple heath-flowers! Richlier burn, ye clouds!
Live in the yellow light, ye distant groves!
  'This Lime-Tree Bower My Prison', Samuel Taylor Coleridge (1772–1834)

This extraordinarily attractive bushy plant has immense horticultural merit and grows well anywhere – borders, rock gardens, bog gardens and exposed banks. William Robinson wrote: 'there is no more beautiful shrub than the native Heather in its commonest form'. Varying from almost prostrate to erect, heather can fill many places and makes an excellent spreading shrub. A truly versatile plant, it thrives in poor ground and, although it prefers an acid, free-draining soil (pH below 6.5) with some moisture, it is found from dry heath to the wettest of bogs from sea-level to over 900m/2,950ft. Despite being tolerant of shade, heather flowers most freely in full sun. After flowering, the bushes can be cut back to keep growth compact. Leggy plants are often improved by covering the centre with garden soil in spring to encourage new growth. True heather or ling (*Calluna vulgaris*) is the sole species of this genus, but there are over 400 cultivars; some of the newer varieties have been rendered sterile to force longer periods of flowering.

GROWTH HABIT Reaches about 60cm/24in.

PROPAGATION Heather is easy to grow from the plentiful seed, collected in October or November, dried and sieved, and sown in spring on a peat-substitute and sand mixture in a cold frame. As heather has mycorrhizal associations (fungal symbiosis), cuttings (taken near the base of the current season's growth in late summer) may not be as successful as seeds.

ROLE IN LANDSCAPE Great sweeps of purple cover heaths and moorland in late summer and autumn when this low-growing evergreen comes into flower. It is our most common shrub of heath, moorland and mountain, with twiggy, prostrate or ascending, much-branched stems. But in many areas of Wales and other parts of the UK, a foreign member of

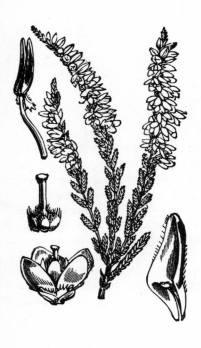

the Ericaceae family, *Rhododendron ponticum*, has escaped and taken over many areas of woodland, causing immense harm to the native flora.

TRUNK, BARK AND BRANCHES
The leafy shoots, which have no prickles, are ascending or erect and round. The bark is ridged, not peeling, and a dark orange-red to brown in colour.

LEAVES The tiny, leathery, stalkless, green leaves are arranged in opposite pairs and withstand dry weather by rolling up, thus reducing the exposed surface area. Each leaf, with two pointed projections from the base, measures up to 3.5mm and hugs the flowering stems.

BUDS, FLOWERS AND FRUIT The long spike-like clusters of bisexual flowers appear from July to the end of September. They are shaped like open bells, with four purple or pinkish-purple (occasionally white) sepals which are joined at the base, hiding the shorter petals. The berry-like capsules which follow contain abundant, hard, dust-like seeds.

PLANT–ANIMAL RELATIONSHIPS Heather is a vital resource for wildlife in the UK. While the mounds around the base of the plant protect ground-feeding birds, such as wrens, in winter they provide shelter for grass snakes and slow-worms (snake-like lizards) from predators such as kestrels or hedgehogs. Heather is also associated with grouse – the shoots and leaves are part of their diet. Partridges, pheasants, starlings and game devour the heather beetle, which is considered to be a pest. Yellow under-wing moths and great egger moths spin cocoons on heather, and emperor moths lay their eggs around the stems. Many insects, including bees, forage for nectar in the flowers, but the amount secreted is variable and depends on soil type and weather. Some of the new cultivars have buds that never fully open. Insects cannot reach inside the closed, narrow buds to pollinate them so they do not get fertilised. Thus the flowers appear to be on the verge of opening, and retain their colour well into the winter long after normal heather flowers have faded and turned brown. These cultivars are, of course, useless for wildlife.

HISTORICAL AND OTHER USES The pinkish or purple flowers produce an orange dye, once used in tartans. The fibrous stems tie thatch on cottage roofs in Scotland and strengthen wattle-and-daub walls. Heather is also woven into fibres for fencing, basket-making, floor mats, thatching, insulation, brooms, mattress-filling and, as the common names ling suggests, to make fire (see below). Heather is the only wild nectar-rich species growing in abundance in Scotland, so beehives are often sited on the moors before the flowers open in late summer: heather honey commands more than double the price of other honey.

NAME *Calluna* from Greek *kallunein*, to sweep; Latin *vulgaris*, common. Heather is first recorded in Scotland as *hathir* (later *hedder*) in the fourteenth century. By the eighteenth century, the word heather was in use, from the heaths where it so often grows. Ling is from Anglo-Saxon *lig*, fire.

Carpinus betulus (Betulaceae)

HORNBEAM

Let beauteous hornbeams one fair part adorn;
Another cypresses, with judgment shorn,
These mazy windings form a wilderness,
Which hornbeam hedges in true nature's dress,
Along the alley sides their boughs expand:
Like verdant walls the firm espaliers stand;
And while the eyes their various forms delight,
To private walks and shady bowers invite.
  Rene Rapin, 'Of Gardens' (A Latin Poem in
  Four Books, 'English'd by Mr Gardiner' in 1706)

Long-lived, slow-growing and usually trouble-free, hornbeam is one of Britain's most majestic trees. With its broad, rounded crown, its smooth, pale grey bark which sometimes has the sheen of steel, it can be a stunning addition to most gardens. Thriving in almost any soil – although usually found in clay soils in the wild – it is usually grouped in the category of small- to medium-sized trees for parks, streets and lawns. It can be planted as a specimen tree, left to grow naturally, coppiced, or made into magnificent verdant walls when grown as a hedge. With its close growth, it is a good hedging plant, and usually keeps its leaves throughout the winter when cut back, often until the young buds push them off in spring. Hornbeam thrives on heavy clay but grows well on any good damp soil especially chalk, but not soils that are sandy and acid. The best soil is well-drained and moderately fertile. It likes a sunny or part-shaded position.

When in leaf from late spring to autumn, hornbeam is often confused with beech, but the leaves lack the bright polish so characteristic of beech. In areas where there are late spring frosts, hornbeam is generally the hardier of the two trees. As the genus *Carpinus* includes many widely planted hornbeams, especially the Swedish hornbeam, the European hornbeam is often confused with them. A distinguishing characteristic of European hornbeam is the autumn colour of the leaves which are a clear, beautiful gold. In summertime the leaves are dark green, thick in texture and are rarely bothered by fungal diseases or insect pests. At Highgrove, Gloucestershire, a dramatic effect has been created with heavily pruned pleached hornbeams in the French style; however, some critics find these too sharp and bare, preferring the less extreme examples at nearby Hidcote Manor where the trees have been left to grow naturally in all their native grandeur.

GROWTH HABIT A slow-growing tree, in ideal conditions it reaches 15–25m/50–80ft but could well take a hundred years to do so. In small gardens it is often controlled by coppicing or pollarding. Because it does not mind shade, in the mid-twentieth century it was still being used as a frost-resistant soil-improver for under-planting oak.

PROPAGATION Seed formed in tiny nuts is usually ripe by the end of autumn and germinates either the next spring or becomes dormant for a year. After two to three years seedlings should be planted from October to March.

ROLE IN LANDSCAPE Hornbeam is found in oak or mixed woods, often showing signs of having been coppiced or pollarded in the understorey in oak and ash woods. A lowland species, in England it is native only south of a line from the Wash to the Bristol Channel. But it is widely planted in other places as it thrives in cold, barren and exposed hills, often where it is difficult to grow deciduous trees; it is much used on roadsides and as hedging. Old hornbeam coppices can be seen in many woods around London, but fully grown trees are rare. Pollarded hornbeams were a feature of woods on London clay in Middlesex, Hertfordshire and Essex. In Epping Forest, on the Essex edge of London, the hornbeam woods were distinguished by their stunted appearance due to coppicing for winter fuel. William Morris, who spent his boyhood in the area, pleaded for them to be spared, saying, 'Nothing could be more interesting or romantic.' He fought against clearing 'the forest of its native trees to plant vile weeds like deodars and outlandish conifers instead'.

TRUNK, BARK AND BRANCHES Hornbeam bark is pale silvery grey and finely striped with brown and grey. Old trees have a raised network of flat ridges; trunks are deeply fluted and rather irregular or oval in shape.

LEAVES Hornbeam leaves are 8–10cm/3–4in in length with seven to fifteen pairs of lateral veins. They are often confused with beech as both are simple and oval in shape, but hornbeam leaves are slightly narrower and longer, with serrated edges, less shiny than beech leaves. Exquisitely veined, they are dark green above and paler below, turning a gold-like yellow in autumn; the leaves on the lower branches often remain a brownish colour and persist throughout the winter.

BUDS, FLOWERS AND FRUIT Tiny green flowers appear in April, just before the leaves unfurl, and hang in pendulous, unisexual yellowish catkins. The conspicuous yellowish males, about 1.5–5cm/2in long, have orange anthers a little larger than the leafy-looking green female catkins, which have narrow, curved-back bracts and red styles. The latter elongate up to 14cm/5½in after fertilisation and are composed of clusters of small, ribbed nutlets, each about the size of a barley grain and attached to a tiny three-lobed bracteole. Like most plants without nectar, hornbeam relies on wind for both pollination and seed dispersal.

PLANT–ANIMAL RELATIONSHIPS Like most native trees, hornbeams are host to a great diversity of wildlife, including a wide range of invertebrates from the larvae of small moths to aphids and beetles. The flowers provide pollen in spring for foraging bees; the leaves are used by several different miners and caterpillars including the copper underwing and nut-tree tussock caterpillars. Hornbeam fruits – nuts surrounded by a ring of leaf-like bracts – are so tough that they can only be cracked by the beaks of hawfinches, which often flock to them in autumn and winter.

HISTORICAL AND OTHER USES Hornbeam wood, fine textured, hard and heavy, is rated as one of the densest of British hardwoods. It was used for cartwheels, watermill wheels, cattle yokes and, before the introduction of glazed earthenware, milk vessels. In the eighteenth century, Carl Linnaeus noted that it was harder than hawthorn. Now, however, its role is limited to chopping blocks and piano hammers. Two reasons for its lack of popularity with cabinet-makers are its inability to polish well and its tendency to shrink when drying. In earlier times hornbeam was burnt as fuel and to make charcoal; on the Continent the leaves were sometimes given to cattle as fodder. The inner bark was the source of a yellow dye.

NAME Latin, from *caprentum*, chariot, which the Romans made from hornbeam due to its hardiness. The common English name is also derived from the strength of the wood: horn meaning hard, and beam meaning tree. The name *betulus* shows its similarity to birch, to which it is related.

Clematis vitalba (Ranunculaceae)

TRAVELLER'S JOY, OLD MAN'S BEARD

On russet floors, by waters idle,
The pine lets falls its cone;
The cuckoo shouts all day at nothing
In leafy dells alone;
And traveller's joy beguiles in autumn
Hearts that have lost their own.
From 'The Last Poems', A. E. Housman (1859–1936)

Glorious small white flowers with fluffy pom-pom-shaped seed heads which often last until winter give this deciduous woody climber its vernacular name, Old Man's Beard. The only genuine liana in Europe, Traveller's Joy can be grown through hedges, along fences or as covering for a dead tree, in woodland margins, parks and large shrubberies. As it is rampant, much care needs to be taken in gardens to prevent it smothering young plants or getting a grip in open ground. It spreads itself over trees, shrubs and hedges by means of strong twisted leaf-stalks, sometimes forming thick blankets. As in the wild, in gardens it establishes easily where the soil is lime-rich. It grows in sun, semi-shade, even shade, and prefers an alkaline soil. In the sixteenth century, Gerard wrote: 'the beautie of the flowers, and the pleasant sent or savour of the same . . . goodly shewe . . . covering the hedges white all over with fetherlike tops . . .' Three centuries later, William Robinson was equally enthusiastic, describing it as 'falling in graceful folds from trees in many parts of the south of England, having in autumn heads of feathery awns', adding: 'It is well known as a garden plant, and from its rapidity of growth nothing is better adapted for quickly covering rough mounds or bowers . . . It is the only native plant that gives an idea of the "bush ropes" that run in wild profusion through tropical woods.'

GROWTH HABIT In the wild it can develop twisted, jungle-like, trailing stems as thick as a man's wrist, covered with stringy bark. These grow up to 30m/100ft in length and from late April carry compound leaves of three to five pairs of well-spaced, oval, pointed leaflets, each 3–10cm/ 1–4in long, with lobed margins. When the stalks of the leaflets feel the pressure of a neighbouring plant they twine round it, using it as a climbing aid.

PROPAGATION If using ripe seed from the fluffy fruiting heads, sow in late autumn and pot out in spring and plant out during the following autumn or spring. Inter-nodal cuttings can be taken in summer.

ROLE IN LANDSCAPE Traveller's joy trails and scrambles over hedgerows and young trees in woodland, on sand dunes and on quarry waste, but is usually confined to chalk and limestone soils. Where there are no shrubs or trees to climb up, it grows flat against the ground. It is abundant in England, especially Yorkshire in the lowlands south of a line joining the Humber and Dee estuaries; in Wales; many sites across Northern Ireland, and is occasionally found in Scotland. Unlike some other members of the buttercup family, it does not need excessive moisture.

TRUNK, BARK AND BRANCHES While the young stems are soft and downy, old climbing stems are long, woody, stringy, ridged and a paler brown, growing to the thickness of an arm, with strongly grooved bark, light in colour, which tears off easily. The vines are bendy and thin when young, but decrease in flexibility over the years with the increase in girth.

LEAVES The leaves are thin, papery, hairy, bluntly toothed into a serrated edge and pale to dark green in colour, growing in opposite pairs. Both the leaf and leaflet stalks are prehensile and coil around branches. They are also acrid and poisonous.

BUDS, FLOWERS AND FRUIT In July and August fragrant clusters of greenish-white, 4-sepalled flowers appear, each 2cm/¾in wide with masses of stamens round the central group of long, hairy styles. They have the appearance of a typical buttercup flower but with hairy, pom-pom-shaped white-plumed seeds; the long, feathery plume on each seed helps wind dispersal. When in fruit the style becomes fluffy and long.

PLANT–ANIMAL RELATIONSHIPS Traveller's joy is a prodigious producer of seed: each plant can turn out up to 100,000 seeds in a year, mostly eaten by birds before they are spread by the wind. Birds are also attracted to the caterpillars of tortricoid moths which feed on the leaves. The pollen-rich flowers are visited by numerous insects, including hover-flies and bees, both for pollen and the nectar at the base of the filaments.

HISTORICAL AND OTHER USES Long ago the branches were used for making light baskets and the the pliant stems were used to bind bundles of wood. Leaves and flowers were once brewed into a tea, said to be a stimulating tonic and a headache cure.

NAME *Clematis* from Greek *klema*, a vine shoot; Latin *vitalba* from *vitis*, vine, and *alba*, white, referring to its fruits. Gerard is supposed to have given it the name Traveller's Joy in the sixteenth century because when in flower it was said to cheer the hearts of all who saw it.

Cornus sanguinea (Cornaceae)

DOGWOOD

In depraved May, dogwood and chestnut, flowering Judas,
To be eaten, to be divided, to be drunk . . .
  'Gerontium', T. S. Eliot (1888–1965)

This striking shrub justifies its Latin name of *sanguinea* – its blood-red stems add colour to hedgerows and gardens in autumn and winter. Indeed, dogwood is so spectacular that its foliage and berries are used in the cut flower industry. The leaves are veined, and the branches generally shot through, with a blood-red pigment; during the first year of growth a large number of its twigs are also dark red. It grows in sun or semi-shade and tolerates a wide range of soils including those that are cold and wet. It can be planted at the back of a large border or fringing a pond where its winter colour will have maximum impact – the shoots remain dark red throughout the winter if the plant is trimmed each year. As it grows fairly quickly it makes a useful hedging plant, and is often incorporated in hedges of holly, privet, hawthorn, beech and cotoneaster.

GROWTH HABIT It usually remains a shrub, only occasionally reaching 4m/13ft. The branching habit is affected by whatever type of pruning is carried out.

PROPAGATION Dense thickets of sucker shoots (which may spread into open ground unless checked) make for easy propagation as they can be taken and grown on. A better, but slower, way is to gather ripe berries in autumn and early spring and sow them thickly in nursery beds before planting out two to three years later. Only about 40 per cent germinate.

ROLE IN LANDSCAPE Dogwood occurs in hedgerows, scrub and on woodland margins on limestone or base-rich clay soils throughout lowland England north as far as Durham and south Cumbria. It rapidly invades abandoned pastures on chalk soils and although it is sometimes found away from chalk this occurs only in the south and is often a garden escape. It is much planted on motorway banks, e.g. on the M40.

TRUNK, BARK AND BRANCHES Twigs are red, and the leaves, set in opposite pairs, change from reddish-green to a bright crimson in autumn.

LEAVES The oval-shaped, hairy leaves are a dull green, veined crimson in autumn. These opposite, short-stalked leaves are 4–8cm / 1½–3in long, with three to four pairs of veins running from base to tip; they turn from green to purplish-red before falling in October.

BUDS, FLOWERS AND FRUIT Flat-topped clusters of small, creamy-white flowers (sometimes tinged with red) appear in June and July, each with four petals and minute sepals. These are followed by black, pea-sized berries which ripen in September, each containing two stones.

PLANT–ANIMAL RELATIONSHIPS About forty different species of shrubs called dogwoods are found throughout the temperate parts of the northern hemisphere, some more ornamental than others. They all give cover for nesting birds, but only one species is native to the British Isles and has all the properties to attract wildlife and provide food for insectivores such as birds, shrews, bats and other small mammals and frogs. It is a good ground-shelter shrub for a variety of animals and a favoured home for birds, including magpies, robins, starlings, blackbirds, blackcaps, blue tits, long-tailed tits, marsh tits, redwings, song thrushes and hooded crows. Among butterflies, it is home for the adults and larvae of the green hairstreak.

HISTORICAL AND OTHER USES For centuries butchers turned dogwood's tough, durable, thin and flexible wood into skewers, known as 'dogs', to hold meat, especially rolled joints, in shape for cooking. The thin coppiced shoots were made into goads sharpened at one end and used by farmers as animal prods when herding stock. The wood was chiselled into everything from mill cogs, arrows and ramrods to toothpicks, and also turned into charcoal for gunpowder. Young branches are still used in basketry. Berries and seeds, bitter and inedible, were a source of lamp oil and oil for soap-making. A grey-blue dye was obtained from the fruit.

NAME Latin *cornu*, horn, referring to the hard, horny wood; *sanguinea*, blood-red. Quite a few small shrubs were called 'dogwood' because their timber was considered suitable only for 'dogs' or wooden skewers. John Parkinson, *Paradisi in Sole Paradisus Terrestris* (1640; the first handbook of English pleasure gardening) wrote: 'Dogge berry tree is not fit to be eaten, or to be given to a dogge.'

OTHER SPECIES The dwarf dogwood *Cornus suecica*, found in the upland moors among low shrubs, is also considered gardenworthy.

Corylus avellana (Betulaceae)

HAZEL

Upon yon tuft of hazel trees,
That twinkle to the gusty breeze,
Behold him perched in ecstacies,
Yet seeming still to hover,
There! Where the flutter of his wings
Upon his back and body flings
Shadows and sunny glimmerings
That cover him all over . . .
　　'Green Linnet', Samuel Taylor Coleridge (1772–1834)

It is difficult to find another shrub or tree to recommend more for gardens than the bushy, multi-stemmed hazel with its canopy of soft green leaves in spring and summer, and golden catkins in winter. Grown as a hedge, a shrub, a much-branched tree or to flank a path to create an ornamental nut walk, hazel's mass of grey-brown twigs makes it one of Britain's most charming native plants – with the bonus of being the country's only native edible nut tree. Its flowers are the earliest, opening in January; in autumn the leaves turn pale yellow, often lasting on the tree until November while the sweet nuts ripen. Hazel likes well-drained soil but is tolerant of a range of conditions – sun or shade, moist or dry – and a variety of soils, including chalk.

Young hazel whips are planted in rows, protected by plastic spiral guards. Pruning and coppicing can keep the tree manageable in size, letting in light to the ground for flowers such as primroses and bluebells to grow beneath. Careful pruning thickens the tree and makes it safer for nesting birds, but caution is needed not to prune when these visitors are laying their nests or raising their young. For a harvest of nuts the plant must be left unpruned or very lightly pruned in winter. Hazel is one of the most important native species for making woven fencing, hurdles and as a 'living fence'. Using the old method of 'cut and lay', plants are bent or partially cut and interlaced, ensuring that hedges are not bare at the base. The restored medieval garden of Prebendal Manor, Northamptonshire, has a nut walk of hazel planted just ten years ago which is now a splendid sight. A more mature one is at Sissinghurst Castle, Kent.

GROWTH HABIT Up to around 5m/16½ft. Occasionally, as at Braving-ton Hanger, Sussex, it is double that size when treated as a tree.

PROPAGATION In the wild, hazel trees are propagated with the aid of animals that flock to the trees to eat the nuts and void them. Nuts need to be sown 5–7cm/2–2¾in apart and kept cool and moist until spring, when the seed germinates. The seeds should be sown in light, sandy soil; if sown directly into outdoor beds they need protection from rodents and other animals.

ROLE IN LANDSCAPE Widely distributed in the northern Hemisphere in hedgerows, as an understorey in oak and ash woods, or as scrub on a wide range of soils, hazel is found throughout most of Britain except for the Shetland Islands and on more acid soils. Much has been planted over the last three hundred years everywhere from gardens to the steep sides of railway cuttings and woods. Hazel is one of the few taller-growing woody plants that tolerate extreme conditions –they even form 'wood-land' in the Outer Hebrides and ascend to 650m/2,130ft in Atholl. A. E. Holden , *Plant Life in the Scottish Highlands* (1952), described the hazel in the Highlands: 'All along the foot of the sheltering hills where Oak and Hazel flourish on the steep sides and all along the road winding round Loch-an-Eilean . . .'

TRUNK, BARK AND BRANCHES The shiny, often mottled brown bark has light-coloured horizontal pores and can be almost silver-grey on stouter stems, while the pale brown twigs are densely covered with stiff reddish glandular hair with blunt buds.

LEAVES The alternate broad, oval, almost round, leaves are light green in colour and slightly hairy, with an almost wrinkled appearance, with doubly toothed margins and short, drawn-out tips. They are slightly like alder leaves.

BUDS, FLOWERS AND FRUIT From January onwards, small, grey-green cylinders of clustered male flowers open into bright yellow, pollen-filled hanging catkins, sometimes known as 'lambs' tails'. Much less conspicu-ous are the female flowers which appear a little later and resemble brown buds with a small crown of bright red stamens. Hazel catkins are distin-guished from other catkin-bearing trees by two-celled ovaries with two styles. Male and female flowers are borne on the same tree, and the female catkins enlarge after fertilisation to form green leafy capsules. By October these turn into smooth, rounded, brown, hard-shelled nuts, usually grouped in small bunches of one to four, and held in leafy, ragged-edged cups of pale green bracts. The tree can be identified in winter by its small, grey catkins.

PLANT–ANIMAL RELATIONSHIPS

Hazel is host to over seventy insect species. Like the willow, it is one of the earliest sources of pollen for foraging insects, especially sought after by bees. The leaves are a food plant for many moth species. Later in the year the nuts are an edible and nutritious source of protein for squirrels, field mice, dormice and the nut weevil with its long snout. These collect the nuts before they are fully ripe, so if you do not want to share the produce with animals, pick it early. The base and roots also provide food, shelter, warmth and safety, and are often as busy as above with tunnels and various nests. Wild mice and rabbits burrow around and below the tree.

HISTORICAL AND OTHER USES Archaeological remains show that hazel was extensively used in pre-Roman Britain. Hazel wood is tough and flexible, and still has an astonishingly wide range of uses: house building, fencing, sheep hurdles, basketwork, thatching spars, rose arbours, pea sticks, besom handles, arrows and, because of its pliability, fishing rods. Shoots are made into walking-sticks, hurdles and crates. The thatching industry consumes some twenty million hazel spars a year, at a value of around £2 million. A large number of hazel liggers (split rods used for roof ridging) are also sold. Wands from hazel were also once used in the foundation of plaster to strengthen walls, in artists' charcoal and dowsing rods. The seventeenth-century diarist John Evelyn wrote: 'Lastly, for riding switches and divinatory rods, for the detecting and finding out of minerals (at least, if that tradition be no imposture), it is very wonderful, by whatever occult virtue . . . to discover not only mines and subterraneous treasure, and springs of water, but criminals guilty of murder . . .' Seldom of sufficient size to be a traditional furniture wood, hazel is sometimes made into outdoor rustic chairs. The plant has given its name to a number of towns, such as Haslemere, Hazelbury and Hazlingfield. And, of course, the nuts are edible: 'filberts especially, if peeled in warm water, as they blanch almonds, make a pudding . . .' (John Evelyn).

NAME Latin *corylus* from Greek *karoun*, a nut; *avellana* from the name of an Italian town where hazel once grew in abundance. The common name comes from the Old English *haesil*, a head-dress, referring to the green cup that supports the nut.

Crataegus monogyna (Rosaceae)

HAWTHORN

Now there was made fast by the tower wall
A garden fair, and in the corners set
A herber green, with wands so long and small
Railed all about: and so with trees close set
Was all the place, and hawthorn hedges knit
That no one though he were near walking by
Might there within scarce any one spy.
  James I of Scotland, describing the gardens of Windsor Castle
  where he was imprisoned 1413–24

Distinguished by its mantle of sweet-smelling, snowy white or occasionally pink blossom, dense mass of tangled branches and deeply cut green leaves, this hardy ornamental small tree is held in great affection. Not only is it glorious when in full flower, but it supports much wildlife. Gardeners also grow it because of its speed: it can make 3m/10ft in its first four years. It flourishes as a hedge, shrub or tree on all but the poorest acid or very wet soils, even in polluted towns, or exposed inland or coastal sites. Good drainage and a loamy soil with moderate moisture around the roots help it prosper. Tough and extremely hardy, it is easily managed and tolerant of sun or semi-shade and of hard pruning. It withstands pruning at almost any time, although after flowering or late autumn is best in order not to disturb nesting birds or butterfly caterpillars.

Along with hazel, hawthorn is recommended as a main component of rural hedges. Clipped and laid, it was traditionally used to make thorny, stock-proof hedges; it can equally make a dense, luxuriant, intruder-proof garden hedge with its thorny stems and branches that repel both burglars and cattle. Its dark, tangled branches are attractive in winter, especially when still laden with red berries, so it can be grown as a specimen tree with year-round interest.

Local native hawthorn trees are difficult to buy. *Crataegus* is a large genus in the northern hemisphere and there are also many cultivars.

GROWTH HABIT It is so quick-growing initially that it earned the name 'quick'. Usually seen as a small spreading shrub or rounded tree, it is variable in size, usually reaching about 6m/20ft tall or occasionally 9m/30ft. It can be very long-lived, often reaching 250 years old. The ancient hawthorn at Hethel, south of Norwich, is over 500 years old; one near Brecon Ash, Norfolk, is said to be about 700 years old.

PROPAGATION Abundant seed can be gathered from the berries in October, but patience is needed: most seeds take at least eighteen months to germinate. The seed-coat is relatively impermeable, so scarification is often practised to speed up the process. Otherwise, seeds need to be sown in a peat substitute or sand mixture in containers in a cold frame and kept moist in a cool place. After one to two years, between October and March, young trees can be set out in permanent sites. New plants also appear in beds and borders as a result of bird droppings.

ROLE IN LANDSCAPE Common in hedgerows, hawthorn remains the most widely planted hedging shrub. Due to its extraordinary qualities as a stockproof barrier, an estimated 200,000 miles of it was planted during the Enclosures in the eighteenth and nineteenth centuries. It is also found in woodland margins and scrub on all but the poorest soils, up to about 500m/1,800ft. It was supposed to be sacred, and there was a tradition (completely without historical evidence) that it furnished Christ's crown of thorns. An early flowering variety, the Glastonbury Thorn, blooms at Christmas: legend says it grew from the staff of Joseph of Arimathea when he thrust it into the ground during a visit to Britain in the first century AD.

Although hawthorn is only one of the plants of May Day, heralding the most significant month for vegetation, it has taken on the name of May. A sprig of hawthorn was chosen by Henry VII (1457–1509), victor of Bosworth Field, as his heraldic device because the crown of the defeated Richard III (1452–85), or a small crown device from his helmet, was found under a hawthorn bush after the battle – hence the saying, 'Cleve to thy Crown though it hangs on a bush.' Much superstition once surrounded this tree and it was considered unlucky to bring hawthorn into the house.

TRUNK, BARK AND BRANCHES When young, the bark on the irregular-shaped trunk is smooth greenish-grey or greenish-brown, but with age it becomes gnarled and twisted and develops distinct flutes; it is rough, slightly flaking and a darker, reddish-grey. The zigzag shoots are covered with short spines.

LEAVES Bright green delicate leaves up to 5cm/2in long unfurl in April, each deeply lobed, becoming dark green above and paler below. They are more or less oval in shape and divided into three to seven lobes, mostly dissected near the midrib.

BUDS, FLOWERS AND FRUIT Showy, aromatic, white flowers, carried in flattish clusters, with up to twenty pink anthers and a single style, are bisexual, with five sepals, five petals and many stamens. They bloom from March to June. The glossy, fleshy, single-seeded fruits, or haws, produced from May to September, turn dark red in autumn, look spectacular in varying shades of crimson, and can last well into January in a mild winter. An old country saying claims that if birds start to feed on the berries in autumn it will be a very cold winter – the implication is that Nature bestows a heavier crop to provide more food in adverse conditions. The claim includes other species, such as holly.

PLANT–ANIMAL RELATIONSHIPS One of the most important shrubs for wildlife, hawthorn provides food for up to 150 insect species, including beetles, leaf-hoppers, sawflies and hawthorn shield-bugs. Many different species of birds eat the insects, and some use the dense bushes as nesting and roosting sites (hawthorns should be left to grow up as trees at intervals along hedges for this reason). Most British land birds are territorial, so the easiest way of estimating the bird population of a hedge is to count the singing males during the breeding season – the dawn chorus in hedges is loudest during the first half of May, and hawthorns provide attractive perches for singing birds.

Hawthorn leaves, along with cowslip and primroses, are host to one of Britain's rarest butterflies, the Duke of Burgundy. The gold tail moth lays its eggs there, brushing its tail over the new eggs to protect them with fallen gold hairs. Other moths include the larvae of the green-brindled crescent, grey dagger, figure-of-eight, mottled umber and yellow-tail – all of these feed singly on the leaves or form communes in webs. The smell of the flowers lures insects including nectar-feeding flies, but the nectar flow is unreliable and some modern, double-flowered cultivars have no nectar. The nutlets in the haws ripen in August, ready to provide autumn and winter food for small mammals, including wood mice and 23 species of birds. Flocks of migratory fieldfares and redwings feast on them when not challenged by blackbirds, mistle thrushes, song thrushes and waxwings. By late winter most haws have been eaten, and the birds have repaid the tree by dispersing its seeds far away.

HISTORICAL AND OTHER USES The dense, pinkish wood makes an excellent, slow-burning fuel; according to Mrs Grieve, *A Modern Herbal* (1931), it made 'the hottest wood-fire known and used to be considered more desirable than Oak for oven-heating. Charcoal made from it has been said to melt pig-iron without the aid of a blast.' Formerly, the timber was used for wood-engravers' blocks, tool handles and small articles; the root-wood was also used for boxes and combs.

NAME Latin *Crataegae* from Greek *kratos,* strength, supposedly because of the hardiness of the wood. The common name originates in the Old English *haga,* hedge, which is thought to come from *haw* or *haig*, berries (though there is some conjecture as to which name came first, berries or hedge). One of its many names, May, is because it was in flower during spring festivities such as May Day.

OTHER SPECIES There are around fifty species of hawthorn, all confined to the north temperate zone, but only two are native to Britain, this and the Midland hawthorn (*Crataegus laevigata*) which is usually found only on heavy clay in central and southern England, and is more suited to shade. It differs in many ways from common hawthorn: it has larger flowers, up to 2cm/5in in diameter; dark red fruit, cylindrical with one nut; twigs that are less thorny and less stiff, and leaves that are larger with short blunt lobes and finely toothed margins.

Cytisus scoparius (Fabaceae)

BROOM

You are all aware that
On our throne there once sat
A very great king who'd an Angevin hat
With a great sprig of broom, which he wore as a badge in it,
Named from this circumstance, Henry Plantagenet . . .
  'The Ingoldsby Legends (The Brothers of Birchington)', R. H. Barham, 1837

A small, bushy, hardy leguminous shrub, broom thrives in any but the shallowest chalky soil, and grows well in gravel beds or on thin dry soils. In the eighteenth century, it was so sought after for gardens that large numbers were dug up in woods and sold in the streets of London. Recently, many local authorities have started planting it on road verges, and some landscape gardeners use it architecturally. Like other legumes, broom helps to enrich soil fertility by adding nitrogen gleaned from the air. Legumes are nitrogen-fixing factories, gathering minerals and trace elements by means of bacteria in root nodules. Nitrogen is a vital plant nutrient – the linchpin in many biochemical molecules, including all proteins, amino acids, chlorophyll and DNA. As nitrogen is essential to plant growth, no garden should be without some sort of leguminous plant – whether it be shrubs such as broom or gorse, clover, alfalfa or peas for the table.

Although broom does not flower until its third year, its thin, straight, twiggy branches and foliage can add interest to shrub borders. It dislikes shade and calcareous soils and thrives best in full sun on free-draining, preferably acid, soil. Young plants develop quickly and turn into decent specimens within five years, but they may not survive very cold winters. Older branches die back, some falling to the ground and rooting.

ROLE IN LANDSCAPE Broom is easy to spot in spring when its dazzling yellow flowers cover the whole bush in a yellow glow. It is widespread on light, sandy, acid heaths, scrub and woodland margins throughout Britain, reaching about 450m/1,475ft in the Lake District. It is never found in heavy shade, but only in the open around the edges of woods. As it likes poor, lime-free soils, it often colonises sand dunes, heaths and open ground in conifer woods, and is also often found on disturbed soil such as new road cuttings or embankments in new forestry plantings. Disliking

very wet soils, it can survive some drought.

GROWTH HABIT This erect, deciduous shrub grows up to 2m/7ft tall, but its lifespan is no more about 8–15 years. Because it grows quickly when young, its stems are weak; older plants which have bent in the wind are often partly prostrate. When broom has been exported to countries such as Australia, it has invaded thousands of miles of native bushland and challenges ruthless clearing.

PROPAGATION In the wild it produces enormous numbers of hard-coated seeds which, as with most of the pea family, can survive for decades, retaining their ability to germinate. In one test, seed viability was retained by four out of 63 seeds after 81 years of dry storage. Seed collected from ripe pods can be sown in spring in a cold frame or greenhouse, or directly into pots, but germination can be erratic. In areas where broom grows easily, seeds can be sown straight in the ground. As it does not transplant easily, young plants must be thinned out before they reach about 30cm/1ft. Softwood cuttings are usually successful.

TRUNK, BARK AND BRANCHES The wiry, slender and arching stems contrast with the spectacular flowers.

LEAVES Its tiny, deciduous leaves grow on the thin branches along with the flowers.

BUDS, FLOWERS AND FRUIT In April, May and June each shrub produces a mass of large golden-yellow, pea-like flowers, each about 2cm/¾in long and borne singly or in pairs on slender stalks. Once the flowers begin to fade, small green pods appear that eventually turn black-brown, each containing up to 22 seeds. When ripe, on warm days in

September, they burst open audibly, flinging out seeds as far as 4m/13ft. Seeds are often further dispersed by ants, water, grazing stock, vehicles and even human footwear.

PLANT–ANIMAL RELATIONSHIPS Broom is a foodplant for the green hairstreak and silver studded butterfly caterpillars. Adult green hair-streaks are fond of basking on the leaves, while the females, harder to spot, flit around searching for leaves for their eggs. Moths that lay on the leaves include the brocade, broom twigminer, broom-tip, grass eggar and streak. Although broom produces no nectar, the flowers have a trigger mechanism that sprays pollen on visiting bees, especially bumble bees which pollinate it. The pods are host to a two-winged gall-midge. Ants are attracted to the seeds and help distribute them.

HISTORICAL AND OTHER USES Broom stalks were once worn in bonnets by certain clans and families as a badge of recognition on battlefields. It was the plant badge of the Forbes, Gordon, Home, MacKay, MacLachlan, Matheson and Murray Atholl clans, as well as a a favourite emblem of the kings of France. In the Wilton Diptych (National Gallery, London), Richard II is seen wearing a broom-pod collar and robes embroidered with broom pods; even the angels are dressed in clothes highlighted with broom. There is confusion over which species is associated with the family name Plantagenet, either this or the petty whin (*Genista anglica*).

These roles contrast with some of its more prosaic uses – as a broom, for example, its twigs bunched together for sweeping floors or scouring butchers' blocks. Although bitter to taste and containing alkaloids which can, if consumed in large enough quantities, depress the heart and nervous system, young spring shoots were sometimes gathered and cooked. The flowers are edible and still sometimes added to salads. Another use was as a long-lasting winter flower arrangement.

NAME From Old English *brom*, a thorny shrub. In Australia it is known as Scotch broom. It was formerly also classified as a genista and is referred to as such in most European languages.

Daphne laureola (Thymelaeaceae)

SPURGE LAUREL

> ... Of laurel, centaury, and fumeterere,
> Or else of elder-berry, that groweth there,
> Of catapuce, or of the gaitre-berries,
> Or herb ivy growing in our yard, that merry is:
> Pick them right as they grow, and eat them in,
> Be merry, husband, for your father's kin;
> Dreade no dream; I can say you no more.
>   'Prologue to The Nun's Priest's Tale', Geoffrey Chaucer (c.1343–1400)

With its bright, early flowers and striking fruits this small evergreen shrub is more than ornamental, but only thrives in a sunny spot on a calcareous soil. In open beds or borders, with its alternate polished green leaves and drooping clusters of flowers in early spring, it provides year-round interest. One of Britain's few native evergreen shrubs and one of the smallest, it was frequently grown in Victorian gardens, though its blossoms are less attractive than those of its more famous cousin, *Daphne meʒereum*. Spurge laurel prefers partial shade or partial sun and often thrives when planted under taller trees. It likes alkaline soils, although in cultivation it tolerates acid soils, even clay. The poet James Fenton wrote: 'When a truly distinguished plant adopts your garden, it is flattering. The wild Spurge Laurel, *Daphne laureola*, brought along by a friend who was ditching nearby, has become a presence for us. One might think it wouldn't like our clay. One would be wrong. It turns up everywhere, a harmonious, low evergreen daphne' (*Guardian*, 7 April 2001). It should be kept away from areas where it might be trodden on or damaged, as it does not regenerate easily.

GROWTH HABIT Inclined to a bushy habit, spurge laurel grows between 1m/39in and, at the most, 1.5m/5ft.

PROPAGATION Germination from seed can be erratic, and only a few seedlings may appear. If propagated with heeled cuttings, these should be taken in late July or August, potted up and grown on in a sheltered, shady spot before planting out in the second autumn or following spring. It is often raised by nurserymen as grafting rootstock for *Daphne* cultivars.

ROLE IN LANDSCAPE It is found on or near chalk south of London, and is widespread in beech and other open, mixed woods and along woodland margins throughout England, but is rarer in the west. In Ireland and Scotland it has been planted or is a relic of shrubberies.

TRUNK, BARK AND BRANCHES Tough and flexible, it easily splits lengthways into long strips. The light greenish-brown corky layer separates easily into papery fragments.

LEAVES With their deep green glossiness and slightly leathery texture, the broadly spear-shaped leaves with entire margins are almost exotic in appearance.

BUDS, FLOWERS AND FRUIT From early February to April, closely packed yellowish-green tubular flowers with radiating petals and sepals are borne in clusters of five to ten in the axils of the upper leaves. Each has four pointed, wide-open petals and in mild, moist conditions emits a strong fragrance. The pistil forms egg-shaped berries which are green at first, but shiny black in late summer. Each contains one hard seed.

PLANT–ANIMAL RELATIONSHIPS The nectar and pollen appear early in the year, in late winter, and are sought after by early moths and bumble bees. Although the berries are toxic to man, they are relished by a variety of birds from finches and warblers to pheasants and grouse.

HISTORICAL AND OTHER USES Occasionally, the bark was turned into quills and was also once used in pharmacies, especially in Russia against the bites of snakes and other venomous creatues. In Siberia an extract treated cracks in horses' hooves.

NAME Latin *laureola* from its similarity to laurel, used by the ancient Greeks to make the crown for the victor in their games. Daphne, daughter of Peneus, was transformed into what is usually assumed to be *Laurus nobilis*, bay laurel, so that she could escape from pursuit by Apollo.

Daphne mezereum (Thymelaeaceae)

MEZEREON (DAPHNE)

'Tis sung in ancient minstrelsy
That Phoebus wont to wear
The leaves of any pleasant tree
Around his golden hair;
Till Daphne, desperate with pursuit
Of his imperious love,
At her own prayer transformed, took root,
A laurel in the grove.
    'The Russian Fugitive', William Wordsworth (1770–1850)

With its fragrant clusters of bright lilac-coloured blossom, mezereon is one of the most attractive of Britain's native shrubs, and is often grown in borders near a house to allow visitors to smell its intoxicating scent. In winter, the pink-mauve tinge of the flower buds on its thin spindle-like branches provides interest until the deep pink flowers take over. Although mezereon grows best in drained, moisture-retentive, mulched calcareous soils with some shade during the hottest part of the day, like all shallow-rooted trees it needs protection from strong winds. It does not respond to pruning and can have a very short life, dying suddenly and inexplicably.

GROWTH HABIT Mezereon reaches about 1–1.5m/3–5ft in height and width.

PROPAGATION Germination from fresh seed can be chancy, taking anywhere between a few weeks to five months. Once rooted, plant it out into a permanent position. If grown from tip cuttings, these should be taken in midsummer and put in a cool spot in a glass house such as underneath a bench, or in a box under a sheet of glass.

ROLE IN LANDSCAPE This hardy shrub grows wild in a few limestone districts, mostly in scrub and woodland, but only as far north as Yorkshire and Lancashire. In other places it is planted. The first record of it was near Andover, noted by Philip Miller, plantsman in charge of the Chelsea Physic Garden and author of the greatest gardening handbook of

the eighteenth century, *The Gardener's Dictionary*. In 1759, Gilbert White wrote enthusiastically about the daphne he found near Selborne.

TRUNK, BARK AND BRANCHES Woody, upright twigs.

LEAVES Small, long leaves, narrowly oval with pointed tips and a dull greyish green, appear at the end of the branches after flowering, forming clusters 1.5–7cm/½–2¾in long.

BUDS, FLOWERS AND FRUIT *Daphne mezereum* has small, fragrant, purple-pink to lilac tubular flowers with spreading lobes which form in the axils of the previous year's fallen leaves. There is a long delay between the formation of the blooms in June and their flowering the following spring. The flowers are followed by bright globose and fleshy scarlet berries (similar to redcurrants) containing seeds which, like all parts of this plant, are poisonous to man.

PLANT–ANIMAL RELATIONSHIPS The seeds are poisonous, but birds eat the berries.

NAME From Persian *mazariyun*, a species of daphne.

Empetrum nigrum (Empetraceae)

CROWBERRY

A good ground-cover plant that suits open, sunny situations, this evergreen shrub creeps across the ground rooting itself at intervals. Low-growing, it has tiny narrow leaves and flowers that grow in the leaf axils early in the spring, when the plant appears reddish in colour. It can tolerate slightly acidic, peaty soils but not very wet areas.

GROWTH HABIT To 15cm/6in tall, with branches up to 40cm/16in long.

PROPAGATION Both male and female plants must be grown if seed is required. Seeds are slow to germinate, and need stratification. When the seedlings sprout, their pots need to be left in a greenhouse for a full winter before planting out in late spring, after any frosts.

ROLE IN LANDSCAPE Widespread on the Scottish hills, crowberry is found across Scotland from the coast to the mountains and in northern England on heaths. It grows with heathers and associated plants on open moorland, but in some areas becomes the dominant species. It prefers drier areas, so is also often found where broom and blackthorn prosper.

TRUNK, BARK AND BRANCHES Young twigs are reddish.

LEAVES Needle-like, 3–8mm/⅛–¼in long with edges rolled under.

BUDS, FLOWERS AND FRUIT The purplish-crimson flowers appear in May and June. The female plants bear small green berries, which turn black when ripe, and contain six to nine nutlets, which are edible but far from delicious.

PLANT–ANIMAL RELATIONSHIP Birds and foxes eat the fruit with its many small seeds. The flowers are visited by pollinators – bees, flies and butterflies – and other insects, including the rare black mountain moth and the burnet moth found on hills near Braemar in Scotland.

HISTORICAL CONNECTIONS AND OTHER USES The plant badge of the Cameron, MacFarlane, Maclean of Duart, Pennycross, Drimn and MacNab Clans. A purple dye is obtained from the fruit.

NAME The name 'crowberry' was first recorded by Gerard in 1597. Similar names in Germany and Scandinavia confirm that the fruit is relished by crows.

Erica cinerea (Ericaceae)

BELL HEATHER

I play'd with you 'mid cowslips blowing,
When I was six and you were four;
When garlands weaving, flower-balls throwing,
Were pleasures soon to please no more.
Through groves and meads, o'er grass and heather,
With little playmates to and fro,
We wander'd hand in hand together;
But that was sixty years ago.
    'Love and Age', Thomas Love Peacock (1785–1866)

With its tight, neat habit and long flowering season, this small, low-growing evergreen shrub is excellent as ground cover or to form mounds in rock gardens or raised beds. From summer through to autumn, delightful small, showy, reddish-purple bell-shaped flowers smother its crown. As bell heather is drought-tolerant, prefers acid soil and thrives in dry conditions, it is best planted in large groups in well-drained, open, sunny areas, but it will grow in semi-shade. In the late eighteenth century, at a time when new species of *Erica* were arriving from abroad, Philip Miller recommended three of the native varieties for gardens: 'notwithstanding their Commonness, yet they deserve a place in small quarters of humble flowering shrubs, where by the beauty and long continuance of their flowers, together with the diversity of their leaves, they make an agreeable variety'.

GROWTH HABIT The erect, branching stems reach 45–60cm/18–24in.

PROPAGATION As always, it is better to grow plants from seed. With bell heather, this involves drying the dead flowers and rubbing them through a fine sieve to extract the seeds, then sowing them in spring in a green-house or cold frame. If purchasing seed, beware of sterile cultivars. Bell heather can also be propagated by layering or from cuttings taken in late summer from the current year's growth. Once rooted, it can be set out in nursery beds the following spring.

ROLE IN LANDSCAPE The sight of hillsides glowing with purple bell heather is unforgettable. It is often found on dry lowland heaths and moors in Scotland and up to 600m/1,970ft in north Yorkshire, but is absent from large areas of the Midlands. It thrives only on acid soils below 6.5pH.

TRUNK, BARK AND BRANCHES Narrow, needle-like leaves are grouped in whorls of three on wiry, hairless stems.

LEAVES The shiny, dark green linear leaves have rolled-back margins and are grouped in whorls of three up to 7mm/¼in long.

BUDS, FLOWERS AND FRUIT The racemes of bell-shaped flowers 5–6mm/¼in long and purplish-red, appear between July to the end of September, in open clusters towards the stem tips. In autumn, once the flowers die the seed capsules ripen. Many gardeners do not dead-head the flowers, since they provide food for birds and also act as a natural way of regenerating the plant.

PLANT–ANIMAL RELATIONSHIPS Bell heather is the foodplant of a moorland moth, the true lover's knot, and the impressive emperor moth (which also feeds on bramble). The nectar-filled flowers attract bees, butterflies and solitary wasps – if the flowers are too narrow for their heads, they bore in from the side and bypass the pollination mechanism. The low-growing mounds protect ground-feeding birds such as wrens and are less prone to grazing by rabbits than common heather. Moorlands are a stable home to a range of wildlife including adders, lizards and slow worms, and small mammals such as voles and mice, which provide a plentiful food supply for owls and other predators.

HISTORICAL AND OTHER USES See entry for heather (*Calluna vulgaris*).

NAME From Greek *ereike*, to break, either because of its alleged medicinal property of dissolving stones in the urinary system, or because its brittle branches break easily. (The girl's name Erica is the feminine form of Erik and has nothing to do with this plant.)

OTHER SPECIES Other gardenworthy species included cross-leaved heath (*E. tetralix*); Cornish heath (*E. vagans*); Dorset heath (*E. ciliaris*); Mackay's heath (*E. mackaiana*); Irish heath (*E. erigena*) and heather (*Calluna vulgaris*).

Euonymus europaeus (Celastraceae)

SPINDLE

. . . And after Autumn past – if left to pass
His autumn into seeming-leafless days –
Draw toward the long frost and longest night,
Wearing his wisdom lightly, like the fruit
Which in our winter woodland looks a flower.*
*The fruit of the Spindle-tree (Euonymus europaeus).
'A Dedication', Alfred Lord Tennyson (1809–92)

A fast-growing decorative but hardy shrub, spindle is often grown for its stunning foliage, berries and autumn colours of yellow, russet and red leaves and vivid pink-and-white seed pods. In contrast to the blossoms, which are not noticeable as they are a similar green to the leaves, the seed vessels in autumn make a spectacular appearance – when ripe they open to reveal seeds a rich yellow in colour. Whether a free-standing tree, a shrub or part of a hedge, spindle is easy to grow. Although it prefers lime-rich soils, it thrives in sun or light shade and adapts to most soils. It is often confused with the Japanese *Euonymus japonicus*, which is evergreen, but fruits only in exceptional summers.

GROWTH HABIT The maximum height is about 1.8m/6ft.

PROPAGATION Best grown from seed, sown as soon as it is ripe, and kept in a cold frame until germination in the second year. Node cuttings can be taken in autumn.

ROLE IN LANDSCAPE Spindle, seldom more than an inconspicuous bush in the wild, occurs in woods and scrub, mainly on calcareous soils, mostly in lowland England. It is seen occasionally north of the line joining the estuaries of the Humber and Dee.

TRUNK, BARK AND BRANCHES Younger twigs are green and squarish in cross-section. As they grow older, they develop brown, corky ribs along the angles, and the stems become round, with smooth, grey-brown bark.

LEAVES Bluish-green opposite leaves are 3–8cm/1–3in long, elliptical or lance-shaped with a pointed tip and finely toothed margin. While the native spindle sheds its leaves in autumn, the Japanese spindle, although closely related, retains them.

BUDS, FLOWERS AND FRUIT In May, loose clusters of small, four-petalled, greenish-white flowers appear in the leaf axils. Together with the green twigs, these blend with surrounding foliage until October. Then female flowers develop into deep pink seed pods that split into four lobes, exposing the orange-coloured aril that surrounds the small, white, pink-coated poisonous seed.

PLANT–ANIMAL RELATIONSHIPS Cross pollination is effected by insects including St Mark's flies which are attracted to the rich nectar source secreted in the fleshy disc surrounding the base of the style. The fruit is eaten by a variety of birds. While the leaves can support the caterpillars of the holly blue butterfly, the fruits provide winter food for small birds, especially robins and tits who enjoy the nutritious pulp of the fruit but usually discard the seed itself. Gardeners should be aware that spindle is the winter host of black-bean aphid and that the berries are poisonous to mammals.

HISTORICAL AND OTHER USES The smooth, hard, whitish wood was traditionally used for making spindles, butcher's skewers, distaffs and other domestic objects such as pegs and knitting needles, as well as musical instruments. Like willow, it makes high-quality artist's charcoal. The pulp of the arils yields a yellow dye or, when mixed with alum, a green dye.

NAME From its use in making spindles.

Fagus sylvatica (Fagaceae)

BEECH

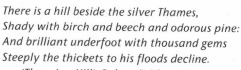

There is a hill beside the silver Thames,
Shady with birch and beech and odorous pine:
And brilliant underfoot with thousand gems
Steeply the thickets to his floods decline.
'There is a Hill', Robert Bridges (1844–1930)

A noticeable feature of this glorious tree is its fresh, springtime canopy of young, almost translucent, pale green leaves. One of England's most handsome and easily recognised trees, beech grows in sun or semi-shade and a wide range of free-draining soils, including chalk. Although when in suitable soil it grows rapidly, becoming too big for a small garden, it is often cultivated as a hedge. Growth can be inhibited as it can be clipped closely. As with all hedges, the length of the roots depends on the frequency and extent of the trimming. Beech has the advantage of tolerating shade and also of building up a great depth of rich humus from its annual fall of leaves.

When trimmed close, beech hedges give much shelter. While most deciduous trees shed their leaves with the advent of winter, shrivelled brown leaves will stay on a well trimmed beech hedge, persisting until they are pushed off by new leaves the following spring. Flowers and leaves of young plants can be damaged by severe frosts, but once established the plant is hardy and drought-tolerant. Like most trees in deciduous woodland, it is tolerant of various light conditions. Growth of ground flora is inhibited because big beech trees get all the water near the surface, and in summer they form a lofty canopy that allows only a pale light to filter to the ground. After a storm, however, when large trees have been knocked down, seedlings get established in the gaps. Being shallow-rooted, beeches can suffer in great storms more than other species. While beech can grow under the shade of any native tree except for yew, few plants grow in its dense shade, apart from bluebells and wood anemones at the beginning of the spring before the leaves have fully opened.

Massive, with a large, dense crown, beech is outstanding for its beauty and is generally regarded as one of the stateliest of England's trees. Vita Sackville-West likened the smooth, green-grey trunks to 'stone-grey columns' in a cathedral, and described its visible strong roots near the surface as 'the knurly tangle of roots that coiled above a scarp like serpents'. She also enthused about the pleasure of walking through drifts of leaves in autumn 'where underfoot the beechnuts split with crisp crackle . . .' Beech has inspired descriptions and verse by many writers. In his poem 'Weathers', Thomas Hardy described 'When beeches drip in browns and duns . . .' Richard Jeffries recalled them standing 'at the edge of the slope, huge round boles rising from the mossy ground, wide fans of branches, a shadow under them, a greeny darkness beyond. There is depth there – depth to be explored, depth to hide in.'

GROWTH HABIT Reaching 30m/98ft, with a girth of about 6m/20ft, sometimes more, older beech trees have a massive multi-branched dome. The rate of growth is around that of oak, but beech does not live for so long – 300 years is generally its limit.

PROPAGATION In the wild, pollination is by wind and the seed is distributed by animals and birds that flock to feed on it. For gardeners and foresters, propagation is by gathering seed. The seed becomes ripe in October, and can be obtained by spreading large sheets around the base of the tree, then shaking the branches violently. Once gathered, seed needs to be planted out in nursery beds protected from mice. The seed crop is variable – one year there can be plenty, the next very little – and many of the seeds might be useless. One old way of sorting seeds is to put them in a tub half-filled with water: as with eggs, the good ones sink to the bottom and the bad float to the top. Suitable seeds should immediately be spread out to dry as they are short-lived, not remaining viable for longer than a year. Sowing is usually done at the end of March or the beginning of April; until then they are often stored in sand. Once in a bed they are left undisturbed for a year, then thinned out and left for another one to two years before final planting.

ROLE IN LANDSCAPE Beech often prospers on thin soils as its roots spread widely but not deep. Found on chalk and limestone uplands and on slightly acid sandy soils, it belongs to the same family as the oak and, like oak, it often dominates its surroundings, taking over from other trees. Beech is native only in southern England, but has been so widely planted that the precise limit is difficult to define. It is grown right through Scotland as far north as Morayshire; the Stuart, Grant and Fife families were noted tree planters. During most of the summer and autumn, the ground beneath beech is usually bare. As well as lack of light, hindrances to other plants are its strong roots near the surface, and the drip of water from the tips of its leaves.

Burnham Beeches, in the grounds of Lord Grenville at Burnham, Buckinghamshire (Buckinghamshire means 'home of beeches'), is the most famous beech wood in Britain, with over 450 ancient pollards dating back to the sixteenth century. One of the most photographed trees there is the Cage Pollard, so-called because of its hollow structure; it was seen in the film *Robin Hood, Prince of Thieves*. Beech is also found massed on the chalk hills of Kent, Surrey, Hampshire and Sussex, as well as on the Cotswold Hills in Gloucestershire. It was a favourite tree for rookeries.

TRUNK, BARK AND BRANCHES
Edith Sitwell described the 'elephant grey bark' which, with the straight tall trunk, makes the tree easily recognisable.

LEAVES Like many other members of the Fagaceae family, beech has alternate, simple leaves up to 9cm/3½in long with short points, wavy margins and five to seven pairs of parallel veins, prominent beneath. These glisten after rain when the sun shines through the trees. In April the brown leaf-scales fall away, revealing emerald leaves clothed in silver down, which take only a few weeks before changing to the

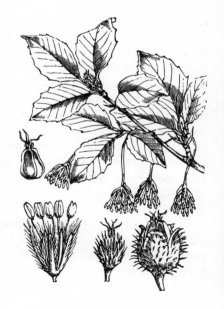

dark green hue they keep until autumn when they become a blaze of orange, russet and gold.

BUDS, FLOWERS AND FRUIT The slender, pointed, pale-brown winter buds begin to expand about the middle of April, the leaves coming out about a week later; flowers appear about mid-May, or a little earlier, but only on trees of at least forty years old. By the first week of June most trees are in full blossom. Male and female flowers are borne in separate catkins on the same tree. The groups of two to three, long-stalked, yellow male flowers hanging from the twigs are quite different from the pairs of greenish female flowers which appear as small, more upright catkins close to the stem. The egg-shaped, downy green fruit ripens into a prickly brown husk in autumn which splits to release two shiny, triangular nuts.

PLANT–ANIMAL RELATIONSHIPS Beech nuts, collectively known as 'mast', are eaten by many mammals and birds, including wood mice, grey squirrels, tits, chaffinches, jays and bramblings. Pigs were let wild in beech woods when there was a heavy crop. The leaves provide food for many moth caterpillars, including the lobster and the least black arches. Grey squirrels hurt the trees by nibbling at the sapwood under the bark.

HISTORICAL AND OTHER USES Beech is as useful as it is beautiful. The fine-grained wood is heavy and comparable in weight to tough oak, making it one of the strongest of the British native timbers. It machines so well that it is the most common hardwood in the British Isles, used for floors, tool handles, bowls, spoons, breadboards, butchers' blocks and small articles such as toys and the high heels for women's shoes. It is highly valued for furniture, especially as it can be steam-bent – beech chairs have been made in the Chilterns for centuries, and in Windsor the Ercol chair is still manufactured, with an elm seat and beech bentwood pieces. Much beech used in Britain today is imported. According to Pliny, ancient Britons mixed beech ash with goat fat to make a bright red dye for their hair and moustaches.

NAME The generic name *Fagus* was used by Pliny in his books on natural history. The common name is from Old English *boc, bece, beoce* – much early writing was carved on boards of beech, which were used as covers for early books.

Frangula alnus (Rhamnaceae)

ALDER BUCKTHORN

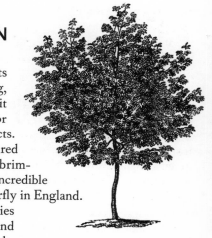

Alder buckthorn, contrary to its name, has no thorns. A charming, deciduous, non-spiny shrub or tree, it is noticeable not for its flowers but for the large yellow butterflies it attracts. Along with buckthorn, it is the favoured foodplant of the caterpillar of the brimstone, which sometimes survives an incredible nine months, the longest-lived butterfly in England. In autumn, when all signs of butterflies have gone, the leaves turn yellow, and violet-black berries appear. Alder buckthorn can be grown singly, in a hedge, in a shrubbery or trained and clipped against a north wall. Although hardy, it does not tolerate drought or a very exposed site, so the wide range of soils in which it grows are usually those with good moisture that are not waterlogged. It grows rapidly after coppicing or cutting back. The Royal Society for Protection of Birds especially recommends it as part of a bird-friendly hedge, along with hawthorn, and 10 per cent each of field maple, barberry, buckthorn, hazel, dogwood or holly.

GROWTH HABIT Alder buckthorn reaches around the same size as common buckthorn, but is less bushy. Its dark grey-brown, ascending branches reach up to 5m/16½ft.

PROPAGATION Seeds, gathered in autumn, stratified and sown in early spring, should be thinned in autumn and grown on before planting in a permanent site two years later. Semi-hard cuttings with a heel can also be taken in late summer, or hardwood cuttings in autumn. Young plants must not be allowed to dry out.

ROLE IN LANDSCAPE Alder buckthorn, found where there are calcareous or damp, acid soils – in open woods, scrub, fenland and bogs throughout most of lowland England – is absent from the north-east and Scotland. It can be seen in Wicken Fen in Cambridgeshire, and also in the New Forest.

TRUNK AND BARK The bark is black.

LEAVES Simple oval leaves are shiny, 2–7cm/¾–2¾in long and set, more or less, in opposite pairs, with parallel veins and untoothed margins. They appear in April.

BUDS, FLOWERS AND FRUIT The inconspicuous, five-petalled, greenish flowers are borne in small clusters at the base of the leaf stalk. These develop into egg-shaped fruits, containing two or three seeds, which turn from green through red to black when fully ripe in autumn.

PLANT–ANIMAL RELATIONSHIPS Alder buckthorn, south of Yorkshire, attracts the yellow brimstone butterfly; in summer the glossy leaves almost glow with the females flying around looking for young leaves on which to lay their eggs. The copious nectar in the flowers means that bees and other insects also visit, as does a tortricoid moth caterpillar which lives on the berries in the summer. In the winter the palatable fruits are a source of autumn and winter food for birds, including mistle thrushes and fieldfares. They, in turn, disperse the seeds which are also stored and eaten by field mice. Goats are known to eat the leaves, so other mammals probably do the same.

HISTORICAL AND OTHER USES For centuries alder buckthorn was coppiced for charcoal of exceptional quality to make slow fuses for explosives; large quantities were gathered in World War One. The bark produces yellow or brown dyes, while the fruit yields green or bluishgrey dyes. Sap green, a dull light-green pigment for watercolour paints, is prepared from the juice of the ripe berries. The bark is also a purgative.

NAME Latin *Frangula*, breaking, from the brittleness of its branches. It was once informally known as the berry-bearing alder.

Fraxinus excelsior (Oleaceae)

ASH

Of all the trees in England,
Her sweet three corners in,
Only the Ash, the bonnie Ash
Burns fierce while it is green.
  'Trees', Walter de la Mare
  (1895–1926)

With its large rounded crown, tall straight trunk and smooth grey bark, ash is one of Britain's most impressive trees. Dense, short-stalked clusters of hanging purple flowers appear on bare twigs in April, before the leaves unfurl, giving the mature ash a purple hue before its feather-like leaves fully open in early May. Once in leaf, its pendulous masses of foliage almost cover the branches which seem to droop and then curve slightly upwards. Long slender seeds remain hanging in bunches through the winter. Unlikely though it sounds, ash can be grown in small gardens as it grows back quickly after cutting; it responds to pollarding and can be coppiced on a cycle every 10–30 years, depending on the desired ultimate size. Although ash grows quickly in a variety of soils, it prospers when planted in moist, well-drained, preferably alkaline soils, but also grows in mildly acid ground. Its hardiness allows it to withstand coastal winds and pollution in towns: it grows surprisingly well in city atmospheres and, being frost-hardy and resistant to many pests and diseases, is excellent in parks and streets. Spring flowers and other species tolerant of semi-shade can grow under it due to its late foliage and open canopy.

GROWTH HABIT Ash usually grows up to around 7.5m/25ft, but in ideal conditions can reach 37m/122ft at maturity, after about 120 years.

PROPAGATION The self-sown seedlings are spread far and wide. Thomas Pakenham, *Remarkable Trees*, wrote: 'every year millions of ash "keys" — long, thin, winged seeds — literally fall by the wayside . . . when they find sanctuary among the thorns of a hedgerow, what elegance they bring to a dull landscape'. In gardens they can also be grown from seeds gathered when still green in early autumn and sown in nursery beds or cold frames. These should germinate straight away, but ripe seeds may need stratifying. Ash is irregular in germination, sometimes growing immediately, but often lying dormant in the soil for about 18 months. After one to two years, seedlings need transplanting and growing on for another two years before setting out in a permanent site.

ROLE IN LANDSCAPE Native throughout Britain, ash is found in woods, scrub and hedgerows, particularly on damp, alkaline soils, mainly on the limestone of the Cotswolds, Derbyshire and Yorkshire. In *Forest Scenery,* William Gilpin called the oak the Hercules of the forest, and the ash the Venus. It is one of the last trees to come out in leaf and one of the first to lose its leaves. Its branches, pinnate leaves and buds are oppositely opposed; it is readily identified in winter by its hard black buds. In marshy situations, the roots grow deep into the ground, acting as drains, hence the old proverb about getting a firm footing: 'May your footfall be by the root of an ash.' The nineteenth-century poet Richard Jeffries described a young ash in *Wild Life in a Southern County* as 'shooting up after being cut, takes fantastic shapes instead of rising straight. The branch loses its roundness, and flattens out to the width of three or four inches, curling round at the top'. It is often difficult to discern which trees are wild and which have been planted. Like lilac, jasmine, privet and forsythia, ash is member of the olive (Oleaceae) family.

TRUNK, BARK AND BRANCHES The smooth, pale-grey bark becomes ridged and fissured with age; in winter the tree can be recognised by its knobbly greenish-grey twigs. Smaller branches tend to droop down and curve upwards at the tip.

LEAVES Deciduous, pinnate, oval or lance-shaped toothed leaves are grouped in pairs on slim branches. Usually there are three to five pairs (occasionally six) on each stem with a single leaf at the tip. They turn yellow before their early fall in October.

BUDS, FLOWERS AND FRUIT The tree, as well as the individual flower clusters and even the separate flowers, can be male, female or hermaphrodite – as the tree may change sex from year to year. Alan Mitchell, one of Britain's great tree experts, said that the ash was a tree of 'total sexual confusion' – sometimes it is unisexual with individual trees bearing only male or female flowers; other times it is bisexual with trees bearing both male and female flowers; sometimes branches bear male flowers one year and only female flowers the next year. Flowers are pollinated by the wind and the large fleshy stigmas mature a few days before the anthers, growing into clusters of flattened blackish fruits with

long, tongue-like wings, known as 'keys', which can remain on the tree throughout winter. The flowers appear before the leaves in April, in loose clusters near the tips of the twigs. They are green in colour, small and inconspicuous, possessing neither calyx nor corolla.

PLANT–ANIMAL RELATIONSHIPS Ash flowers have no nectar, but other parts of this hospitable tree can support 41 species of insects. Its seeds and fruit are an important source of food for small mammals and birds, especially bullfinches, which can show a preference for one particular ash tree – groups of up to twenty will sit on the branches while ignoring surrounding ash trees. Leaf buds are also eaten by birds, including wood pigeons. The moth caterpillars that breed on the tree include the ash pug, buff tips, sallow, copper underwing, dusky thorn, lilac beauty, lunar thorn, privet hawk-moth, purple thorn, brick and coronet.

HISTORICAL AND OTHER USES As ash is the toughest and most robust of British native trees, its timber was part of Europe's prehistoric economy. According to Greek myth, Cupid and the soldiers in the Trojan Wars used ash bows. Whenever timber was needed to take shocks or strains without risk of fracture, ash was chosen – a role now taken over by steel or plastics. This supple and strong timber, split and steamed, was used for wands, spears, walking sticks, hammer heads, oars, billiard cues, cricket stumps, skis, hockey sticks, furniture, ornaments, handles and basket frames. Stronger than oak but not as durable, it often decays unless treated with preservatives such as creosote. During World War One ash was severely depleted in Britain, being used for railway carriages, aircraft, vehicle frames and shovel handles. It was reputed to be the best fuel for a fire, whether green or weathered.

Once ash was thought of as a magic tree, with special properties for healing the sick or crippled children. A form of sugar, known as 'manna', was obtained by making incisions in its bark. Ash and oak, the last tree species to unfurl their leaves in the spring, are both associated with predictions of the coming season's rainfall:

If the ash before the oak
We shall have a real good soak;
If the oak before the ash
We will only have a splash.

NAME Latin *Fraxinus* from Greek *phrasso*, to fence, from the use of ash in fencing; *excelsior* indicates a special tree of greater height. The common name is from Old English *aesc*, which relates to the name in many other European languages.

OTHER VARIETIES The weeping ash (*pendula*), discovered in the nineteenth century in a field at Gamblingay, Cambridgeshire, makes a spectacular tree, especially in a parkland setting.

Hedera helix (Araliaceae)

IVY

Save that, from yonder ivy-mantled tow'r
The moping owl does to the moon complain
Of such as, wand'ring near her secret bow'r,
Molest her ancient solitary reign.
Beneath those rugged elms, that yew-tree's shade,
Where heaves the turf in many a mould'ring heap,
Each in his narrow cell for ever laid,
The rude forefathers of the hamlet sleep.
  'Elegy Written in a Country Churchyard', Thomas Gray (1716–71)

Few plants have so many uses in the garden as this versatile evergreen climber which can be used as ground cover in dense shade, as a covering for a wall or an old tree stump, as a frieze at the base of stonework, or trailing from a container. Ivy flourishes where little else will grow, and climbs to great heights by means of small clusters of sucker-like outgrowths. When used as ground cover, some gardeners control it by mowing with the blades of a rotary mower set high. Although many different ivies are available, *Hedera helix* is the only form that regularly flowers and fruits in Britain, and grows in almost any position and on almost any soil. In town gardens it is resistant to pollution.

Contrary to much advice, ivy does not harm healthy trees as long as it does not cover the crown. It is not a parasite and does not harm the plants on which it climbs, but it should not be planted close to young trees because it will compete for moisture and nourishment while they are becoming established. Some people believe that ivy loosens the mortar on walls as it penetrates; others, notably in Paris, think it does no damage if the bricks or stone and mortar are sound. Overgrown plants can be cut back hard in spring. Flowering shoots can be affected by severe frosts.

GROWTH HABIT Its woody stems almost bond themselves to stones and trunks and can climb up to 30m/98ft. If there is no support for the masses of short rootlets along the stem it will scramble along the ground.

PROPAGATION Germination from collected seed can be erratic, but seedlings spread by birds will often appear near established plants and

these can be pulled up and grown elsewhere. Young plants prefer a short run across the ground before climbing. The easiest way to propagate this robust plant is from naturally formed layers or from cuttings taken in late summer, grown on in a shady spot and planted out a year later.

ROLE IN LANDSCAPE Because it is a dense evergreen, ivy is distinctive in winter when trees have shed their leaves and it is seen growing up tree trunks.

TRUNK, BARK AND BRANCHES Ivy's stout stems are covered with brown rootlets by which it attaches itself to its host.

LEAVES Dark, leathery, lobed, glossy leaves change their shape as the vine climbs and reaches maturity. Those near ground level, where they have scant light, are generally dark and almost star-shaped – with five distinct, triangular lobes when not in flower, and three lobes when in flower. Those on the higher, flowering shoots are transformed when the plant reaches the light, where it bears uncut oval or wedge-shaped leaves.

BUDS, FLOWERS AND FRUIT Ivy is one of the few plants to come into flower late in the year. Even in deep shade ivy continues to climb, but it requires appreciably more light to induce it to bloom. From September to November it produces eye-catching greenish-yellow, globular, stalked heads of tiny, five-petalled flowers with five prominent stamens. Later, if pollinated, these flowers are followed by clusters of leathery berries, each black and glossy, and each containing up to five whitish seeds.

PLANT–ANIMAL RELATIONSHIPS Once ivy has gained height and thick-ness, it is one of the most hospitable of all English plants for wildlife, providing a home for a wide range of invertebrates. Cross-pollination is effected by insects crawling in and out of the flowers. Ivy provides over-wintering sites for the brimstone butterfly which relies on the nectar before it hibernates; the holly blue lays its second brood on the flower buds. The leaves are the foodplant of the swallow-tailed moth; other moths feed on the nectar at night, especially the green-bridled crescent, the swordgrass and the beaded crescent. By day the nectar nourishes wasps, hoverflies and butterflies. In late autumn and winter the black berries are eaten by blackcaps, fieldfares, redwings, robins, wood pigeons, blackbirds and thrushes. The dense cover that mature ivy creates on trees and walls is also invaluable for birds as a nest-site in summer and as shelter in winter, especially for wrens. In autumn it often provides a base for groups of noisy sparrows, sometimes thirty or more on one plant.

HISTORICAL AND OTHER USES A black dye was once made from the berries.

NAME *Hedera* and *helix* are from Celtic words meaning cord and to encompass. The English name is supposedly derived from a Celtic word meaning green or from Old English *ifig*.

Helianthemum nummularium
(Cistaceae)

ROCKROSE

A huge crag-platform, smooth as
   burnish'd brass
I chose. The ranged ramparts bright
From level meadow-bases of deep grass
Suddenly scaled the light.
Thereon I built it firm. Of ledge or shelf
The rock rose clear, or winding stair.
My soul would live alone unto herself
In her high palace there.
   'The Palace of Art', Alfred Lord Tennyson (1809–92)

This short-lived, delicate perennial is now becoming rarer; it was once found in most areas of chalky grassland and calcareous soils in Britain. Sun-loving and low-growing, it thrives in unimproved grassland or where grass is kept short by sheep or rabbits (which also eat the rockrose). It is often grown in gardens for its orange and brown petals; when leggy and overgrown it has to be replaced.

GROWTH HABIT A low-growing, semi-shrub that reaches about 30cm/ 12 in, seldom higher.

PROPAGATION Cuttings can be taken in the summer and the three-valved fruits can also be planted in open, loamy, calcareous soils.

ROLE IN LANDSCAPE Frequent in unfarmed thin soil or on steep slopes, especially chalky grassland, notably in County Durham which contains large areas of limestone grassland, rockrose is found with species such as bird's-foot-trefoil, small scabious, kidney vetch and knapweed.

TRUNK, BARK AND BRANCHES It has a much-branched, straggly, woody stem.

LEAVES Oblong, narrow, green and sparsely hairy on the upper side; white and strongly hairy on the underside.

BUDS, FLOWERS AND FRUIT Yellow-petalled flowers occur in groups of anything from one to three or four, and are about 25mm/1in in diameter.

PLANT–ANIMAL RELATIONSHIPS Flying insects of various kinds visit the flowers and bees appreciate the abundant pollen. Cross-pollination is effected by insects alighting in the middle of the flower and taking the pollen to other blossoms. Caterpillars of several moth and butterfly species live on the foliage, and in certain areas it is a foodplant of the green hairstreak and northern brown argus butterflies (mostly limited to the limestone grasslands of the north of England and Scotland), as well as the wood tiger moth.

NAME From Greek *helios*, sun, and *anthemom*, flower. The common name is derived from its similarity to the wild rose.

OTHER SPECIES White rockrose (*H. apenninum*) is more common in dry limestone grassland, while hoary rockrose (*H. canum*) is found in rocky limestone pastures. The quick-flowering spotted rockrose (*Tuberaria guttata*), a delicate, low-growing flower that blooms in the morning and drops its petals by the middle of the day, is grouped in another species although part of the Cistaceae family. It is found in exposed coastal areas, such as West and South West Ireland, North West Wales, Jersey and Alderney.

Hippophae rhamnoides (Elaeagnaceae)

SEA BUCKTHORN

This trouble-free, decorative deciduous shrub grows easily on sandy soil and is tolerant of sea spray and winds, growing naturally on sea-shores, sand-dunes and cliffs. It can survive a wide range of soil and weather conditions. Apart from being tough and surviving desiccating winds, it has a distinct beauty with silvery-grey foliage and thorny branches, and is one of the few British native plants to have bright yellow-orange or red berries (most wild plants have blue, blue-black or very dark purple fruits). It is also prized for its free suckering, which gives body to loose, sandy soil. As with other leguminous plants, the roots develop small nitrogen-fixing nodules, which add much-needed nitrogen to the soil. It is a suitable and hardy plant for impenetrable hedges, as the spiky branches really are sharp.

GROWTH HABIT Up to about 2m/7ft.

PROPAGATION Easily grown from seed.

ROLE IN LANDSCAPE Sea buckthorn prospers on sandy shores of the east and south-east coasts of Britain, especially on the beaches of East Anglia. It suckers freely, and in Scotland the coasts are covered with mile after mile of it, in some areas forming almost a monoculture. In Galloway, it grows almost to the water's edge, often on white sandy hillocks.

TRUNK, BARK AND BRANCHES While young twigs have silvery scales, the older branches are much-branched, thorny and dark brown.

LEAVES Sea buckthorn's shiny green-grey leaves, which have curious flat-tened brown star-shaped scales, appear after the flowers. Long, extremely narrow and lance-shaped, the leaves look dramatic against the clusters of yellow berries.

BUDS, FLOWERS AND FRUIT The bronze buds are very distinctive while the small greenish flowers at the base of each new shoot are unisexual and inconspicuous. These develop into bright yellow-orange berries clustered on the branches in bunches.

PLANT–ANIMAL RELATIONSHIPS Sea buckthorn forms excellent cover for birds and small mammals. Wind-pollinated, the flowers have no nectar, but the autumn fruits are relished by migrating birds arriving from Scandinavia just as the berries ripen. The berries are edible, but the rest of the plant is poisonous. The sharp prickles afford shelter to nesting birds.

HISTORICAL AND OTHER USES Apart from its value in the fixation of moving sand dunes, sea buckthorn secretes an oil from its seeds and pulp that was once used for the treatment of bedsores and other skin problems. Sea buckthorn berries, which are very acid, are a rich source of vitamin C, and are still used by coast dwellers to make jams and preserves. In Russia it is grown commercially, a practice still in its infancy in Britain.

NAME From Greek *hippos*, horse, and *phaos*, to shine. Sea buckthorn was mentioned by Dioscorides and Theophrastus as a renowned tonic for horses: its leaves and branches were added to horse fodder to encourage weight gain and a shiny coat.

Humulus lupulus (Cannabaceae)

HOP

The sun in the south or else southlie and west
Is joy to the Hop, as welcomed ghest
But wind in the north, or else northerly east,
To Hop is as ill as a fray in a feast.
     Five Hundreth Points of Good Husbandrie', Thomas Tusser, 1573

With its five-pronged yellowish-green leaves and pleasantly fragrant fruiting heads, hop is both attractive and ornate when growing up screens, trellises, small trees, hedges, walls, pergolas and garden fences. It is an excellent alternative to some imported species of clematis. Famous for its small, bitter-smelling female flowers which hang in spike-like infloresences and ripen into fruits similar to fragile yellowish-green papery cones, hop can be a handsome addition to many gardens. A herbaceous perennial, it climbs up anything and maintains its grip with small tendril-like tips; stiff, backward-pointing hairs on the tough, fibrous stem help it make its way through neighbouring foliage. The twining stems, up to 8m/26ft, can also be trained along ropes or on poles. Hop sheds its leaves and stems in winter, making the whole of its summer growth afresh each year from underground stock. It must be firmly supported with wire, stakes or a trellis, so that it grows towards the light, otherwise it spreads along the ground without gaining much growth. Prospering in sun or semi-shade, it prefers moist, well-drained soil but needs to be open to the air so that any excessive moisture is dried up.

GROWTH HABIT With appropriate support, hop will grow in a clockwise direction, twisting as it goes, scrambling up a tree or through a hedge at tremendous speed, reaching 6m/20ft in a single season. If it likes a situation it may well become rampant, the roots penetrating deeply into the soil and the top growth racing away.

PROPAGATION Propagation is by sowing seed under glass in April and planting out in late May or June, or by division in autumn.

ROLE IN LANDSCAPE These deciduous herbaceous perennials scramble up hedgerows, fences, walls, telegraph poles and scrub, and lurk in overgrown thicketed areas in damp soils in the lowlands of southern England. Hops sometimes grow wild at the edge of woodlands or hedgerows in heavy clay soils, but these plants are mostly escapees from gardens or brewery farm, especially around Tunbridge Wells in Kent where there are extensive plantations of hop gardens.

TRUNK, BARK AND BRANCHES The twisting slender stems are tough but not woody, rough to the touch with thick sap and straggly tendrils.

LEAVES With their serrated edges, the small, opposite, three- to five-lobed, vine-like leaves, pointed and almost round, are very attractive.

BUDS, FLOWERS AND FRUIT From July to August the flowers appear, male and female on separate plants. The green male flowers are somewhat inconspicuous with five small petals and stamens. Female flowers have a single-celled ovary and one ovule. The green male flowers are carried in loose, branched clusters, while the tiny, green, egg-shaped, female flowers are hidden by scales. After pollination the scales enlarge into the familiar, papery, yellowish-green cones shielding resinous glands. Lupulin, a substance accumulated in female hop flowers, is the source of the bitter flavour in beer. It comes from nectaries at the base of each bract; the panicles of cone-like fruiting heads enclose nut-like fruits which hang in clusters known as hop. If cones are needed, both a male and female plant must be grown.

PLANT–ANIMAL RELATIONSHIPS The British native hop is the preferred foodplant for the comma butterfly, but the decrease in demand for hops in beer means that the comma is forced to find alternative leaves on which to lay its eggs; it now chooses the stinging nettle as its breeding plant, sharing it with the small tortoiseshell, red admiral and peacock butterflies. Many gardeners grow *Humulus japonicus* or cultivars such as golden hop, but these are unsuitable for the comma larvae. Hop leaves are also sometimes enjoyed by insects including the pale tussock, twin-spotted quaker, pepper and ghost moths.

HISTORICAL AND OTHER USES While the first record of hops in brewing beer was in the ninth century, the first known written treatise dates from the sixteenth century. The rural industry of hop gardens in Britain began in Kent in the reign of Henry VIII (who, like George III, is said to have used hop pillows to induce sleep). At the beginning of the twentieth century around 20,235 hectares in Kent were given over to hops; at the end of August, families and migrant workers plucked the fruit which was taken to oast-houses and dried upon horsehair nets in cones high above charcoal and brimstone fires. William Cobbett referred to the young shoots being cooked and eaten like asparagus in *The American Gardener* (1854): 'To range the Hop amongst Vegetables may appear odd; but, it is a garden-plant in America, and does give you, if you like to have it, a very good dish for the table.' It was also used to make a calming tea and is a sought-after ingredient in dry flower arrangements.

NAME Latin *Humulus*, origin uncertain, but it may have descended from the Low German word *humela*, hop; *lupulus*, of the wolf – Pliny referred to the plant's strangling habit as it climbs, similar to the way a wolf squeezes the life out of its prey. The common name comes from Old English *hoppan*, to climb. Hops once were designated as part of the Moraceae or mulberry family, but have been moved to Cannabaceae, the hemp family.

Hypericum androsaemum (Hypericaceae)

TUTSAN

The large, bright yellow, long-flowering, starry flowers of this shrubby, semi-evergreen deciduous shrub are extremely ornamental, making it attractive in mixed borders. It tolerates a wide range of soils especially those that are rich, loamy, acidic and well-drained, providing there is some moisture; it likes moderate shade where the soil does not dry out. Like other plants in the St John's Wort family, it is noted for its shade tolerance, but too much shade decreases flower production and it prefers full sun. In the summer, wilt and root rot (caused by nematodes) can be a problem, particularly when the weather is hot and humid. Leaf spot, mildew and rust are less threatening. In harsh winters it may suffer tip dieback or die completely, so it is best to mulch around the base of plants.

GROWTH HABIT This low-growing shrub is woody, branched, and usually reaches no more than about 1m/39in in height.

PROPAGATION In winter when plants die to the ground, the roots often survive and send up new shoots, which break through the ground in spring. Tutsan can also be propagated by sowing seed in autumn in a cold frame, by dividing, or by rooting semi-ripe cuttings in summer.

ROLE IN LANDSCAPE Widespread in woodland, in hedge banks on damp, moderately acid to base-rich soils in the lowlands of southern and western England, especially in Devon and Cornwall, it is also found on sea-cliffs. It is scattered only thinly elsewhere and is almost absent from the north-east.

TRUNK, BARK AND BRANCHES The stem is two-edged and a reddish colour.

LEAVES Pairs of smooth, ovate to oblong, purplish-green, stalkless leaves each up to 9cm/3½in long give off a mildly resinous scent when bruised.

BUDS, FLOWERS AND FRUIT From June to August groups of up to nine five-petalled flowers in rose-like clusters with bushy centres of yellow stamens up to 2cm/¾in in diameter appear at the tops of stems. The tufts of the stamens are almost as long as the petals. These attractive flowers are followed in autumn by showy, berry-like fruits which turn from red to purplish-black when ripe, containing numerous oblong seeds.

PLANT—ANIMAL RELATIONSHIPS Though lacking nectar, the bright colour of the flowers and the abundant pollen produced by the stamens attract many pollen-eating and pollinating beetles and other insects.

HISTORICAL AND OTHER USES The dried leaves smell sweetly resinous and have been used as scented bookmarks; they keep their perfume for up to four years. According to Gerrard, the oil obtained from the leaves was the best remedy for 'deepe wounds'.

NAME The common name is from French *tout* and *sain*, meaning all healthy: the fresh leaves had widespread medicinal uses, including the dressing of cuts and grazes.

OTHER SPECIES At least nine other species of *Hypericum* are in cultivation.

Hypericum perforatum (Hypericaceae)

PERFORATE ST JOHN'S WORT

Copious of flow'rs the woodbine, pale and wan,
But well compensating her sickly looks
With never-cloying odours, erly and late;
Hypericum, all bloom, so thick a swarm
Of flow'rs, like flies clothing her slender rods,
That scarce a leaf appears, mezereon, too . . .
  'The Winter Walk at Noon' from 'The Task',
  William Cowper (1731–1800)

This small, delicate, clump-forming perennial shrub is distinguished, like all species of *Hypericum*, by opposite leaves which, due to their oil glands, have a perforated appearance when held up to the sunlight. It has an even longer flowering period than *H. androsaemum*, with numerous flowers as large as tutsan but with smaller leaves and spear-shaped sepals. Tolerating a wide range of well-drained soils in sun or semi-shade, it can be useful in dry shade on chalky soil in borders, on dryish banks, or naturalised in meadows. Handsome examples can be seen, along with other medicinal herbs, at Chelsea Physic Garden, London.

ROLE IN LANDSCAPE Perforate St John's Wort, the most common of the genus *Hypericum* in Britain, prefers rocky slopes, dry grassland, meadows, open woods and hedgebanks, and mainly lime-rich soils.

PROPAGATION Seeds may be sown in a cold frame in early spring, or outside in April. The fine seed germinates more readily on damp soil. It can also be propagated by division or by taking cuttings of the new season's young shoots in late spring or early summer.

GROWTH HABIT Maximum about 1m/3ft in height.

TRUNK, BARK AND BRANCHES The hairless, upright, two-ridged stem has a woody base.

LEAVES Inconspicuous leaves, each paired, elliptical to narrowly oblong and stalkless, are covered with translucent glands looking like punctures.

BUDS, FLOWERS AND FRUIT Bright yellow, star-shaped, five-petalled flowers with pin-cushion stamens appear in widely branched clusters from June to September. These, too, are dotted with glands that show black on the edges of the petals. The almost pear-shaped fruit capsule contains numerous, oblong, pitted seeds and splits into three.

PLANT–ANIMAL RELATIONSHIPS Bee-flies and other insects visit the flowers for their nectar and pollen.

HISTORICAL AND OTHER USES St John's Wort is famous for containing a pigment known as *hypericine* which is used in herbal medicine.

NAME From Greek *hyper*, above, and *eikon*, picture: early Christians placed the flowers above an image to ward off evil spirits at midsummer. Latin *perforatum*, from the marks on its leaves. The common name is from St John's Day, 24 June, when it was picked for ritual and medicinal use.

OTHER SPECIES Slender St John's Wort (*H. pulchrum*) forms a small bush with slender woody stems and pretty, small-leaved foliage, seldom growing more than 15–30cm/6–12in high. Found in the Scottish Highlands but scarce north of Inverness, it is tolerant of a wide range of soils, including quite damp areas, and suits shade. Widely planted, it is often seen in urban areas, especially on rough ground. It tolerates slightly damp soil but is equally at home in drier conditions.

The delicate orange-yellow flowers, which last for many weeks, have five petals which open flat to show off the mass of stamens carrying the pollen, adding to the attractiveness of the blooms. These are followed by large green berry-like seed pods which gradually turn bright red and then black as they ripen, filled with minute, dust-like seed. In sheltered sites, the oval- to spear-shaped leaves may stay green through most of the winter months. Once an ingredient of a Highland wound ointment, twigs of this hardy shrub were also a valued amulet for warding off unwanted bouts of second sight or visions of ghosts. It was the plant badge of the MacKinnon clan, and the source of yellow and red dyes.

Ilex aquifolium (Aquifoliaceae)

HOLLY

Most friendship is feigning,
Most loving mere folly.
Then, heigh, ho! The holly!
This is life most jolly.
Heigh, ho! Sing heigh, ho!
Unto the green holly.
    'As You Like It', Act II,
    William Shakespeare (1564–1616)

Next to yew, holly is the most outstanding evergreen tree in Britain. It grows into a splendid garden tree, but only the female trees carries the small clusters of white flowers and bright scarlet winter berries, which are so associated with Christmas. As male and female flowers are produced on separate plants, trees of different sexes need to be within 30m/98ft of each other so that bees can pollinate the female flowers. Holly tolerates sun and shade – but the greater the light, the denser the foliage. Semi-shade is preferable in midsummer, since heavy shade prevents fertilised holly from bearing fruit and, instead of its usual conical or spire shape, it takes on a straggly appearance.

Holly accepts a wide range of soils from clay and peat to sand and chalk, although it grows largest in rich, sandy loam. It prefers well-drained, slightly acid, soil in open areas, does not like waterlogged ground and is reasonably drought-proof. The prickly leaves take many years to rot down but when dried can be can be scattered round the base of vulnerable shrubs to repel slugs. In the eighteenth century holly was grown with oak in the New Forest to repel animal and human intruders.

If pruning is necessary, it should be done in early spring before any growth begins. Holly is tolerant of clipping and is often trimmed into a fine garden hedge, having the advantages of being constantly green and shining, and an effective barrier against cold winds, noise, pollution, stray animals and burglars. It provides birds with shelter, nest sites and berries. When Peter the Great came to England and worked at Deptford dockyards, he stayed nearby with John Evelyn at Say's Court, and suggested that he grew a holly hedge 'about four hundred feet in length and nine feet high, and five in diameter . . . at any time of the year glistening with its armed and varnished leaves . . .'

William Robinson wrote of holly that 'no country attains the beauty it does in our own . . . Not merely as a garden tree is it precious, but as a most delightful shelter around fields for stock, in paddocks and places which we wish to shelter.' Perhaps similar thoughts of it as a haven inspired Prince Charles to build a tree house for his young sons high in an old holly tree at Highgrove, with a balustrade and door shaped like holly leaves.

ROLE IN LANDSCAPE Native throughout much the British Isles, holly is common in woods, often as part of an understorey in oak and beech woods, in hedgerows and open scrub on a wide range of soils, as far as 500m/1,650ft in West Yorkshire. It grows more vigorously in the milder winters of western Britain, from Scotland south through Lancashire and Wales to Cornwall. Long ago there was a superstition that to cut down a holly was unlucky, so many old species are still standing, especially in hedgerows. Holly woods can be found in Epping Forest, Essex.

GROWTH HABIT Although holly is usually no more than 10m/33ft tall, when grown in an open position it can reach up to 23m/75ft, with a narrow, conical crown, but it is slow-growing.

PROPAGATION In the wild, the trees reproduce themselves through the agency of birds which eat the hard white seeds of the female trees in autumn and winter, so spreading the species over vast areas. The seeds either germinate in the following spring or lie dormant for a year. For gardeners it is more difficult. Holly can be grown from seed, which should be harvested as soon as it is ripe in winter. Once collected, many gardeners rub the fruit through a coarse sieve to separate the seeds from the flesh of the berry, and then stratify them before sowing in a nursery bed where they need protection from birds and small rodents during the eighteen to twenty months they take to germinate. Any cuttings taken with a heel in late summer need to be temporarily planted in a shady cold frame, transplanted after a year and grown on for a further one to two years before setting in a permanent site. Final planting should be in early spring, before any new growth begins. Holly has soft roots and does not transplant well, so is often container-grown.

TRUNK, BARK AND BRANCHES The bark is dark green when very young, becoming steel-grey, smooth, dense and finely fissured. Older trees often have warts.

LEAVES Leathery, highly glossy but prickly, dark green leaves usually last on the tree for two to three years. Unlike deciduous trees which fade and shed their leaves in autumn, holly leaves fall from trees in the spring and do not wither or lose their green colour until on the ground. The lower leaves, and those on younger trees, have wavy margins and stout, sharp prickles; upper leaves and those on older trees can be smooth-edged with a pointed tip. Their shape is oval to elliptical, 5–12cm/2–4¾in long, with a shiny dark green surface but paler underneath. Their waxy surface prevents transpiration of water, allowing the green of the leaves to last through the winter when the ground is often frozen.

BUDS, FLOWERS AND FRUIT In May and June, occasionally also in the autumn, small, fragrant, waxy, white, four-petalled flowers appear in clusters in the leaf axils. Male and female flowers are usually carried on separate trees; occasionally, both sexes occur on one tree. At least one male has to be planted for every six females to ensure pollination. In good years, female trees produce abundant scarlet berries, each containing up to four black seeds, which ripen in late autumn or early winter and often last until spring. The berries can cause upset stomachs if eaten.

PLANT–ANIMAL RELATIONSHIPS As well as giving cover and shelter to small birds in all seasons, holly is hospitable to other animals. In spring, holly blue butterflies lay eggs at the base of flower buds, preferably on female bushes, and the larvae feed on the buds, berries and terminal leaves. In May, nectaries at the base of the flower petals attract pollinating bees. Holly leaves are eaten by two species of tortricoid moths and a leaf-miner. The red berries that appear in October are small enough to be swallowed whole by most fruit-eating birds; they are resistant to extreme cold, and remain fresh with a good moisture content. They can last on trees for almost a year, but are usually eaten by blackbirds, wood pigeons, collared doves, song thrushes, robins, blackcaps, fieldfares and redwings. When snow makes ground-feeding impossible, mistle thrushes defend holly bushes to keep a long-term food supply through winter.

HISTORICAL AND OTHER USES Today, the holly is mainly a source of Christmas decoration, but the strong, compact, white wood was once used for turning, especially in the manufacture of mathematical instruments, chess pieces, harpsichord hammers, butts for billiard cues, and by cabinet-makers for inlay. In the early nineteenth century, knots and burrs were turned into snuff boxes; mallets were made from the rough timber and walking sticks and whip handles were forged from young, straight, quickly grown shoots. Because the wood was so dense, it was stained black as a substitute for ebony as well as being sought after for making pulley-blocks for ships. Due to its fire-resistant characteristics, holly was said to be the safest wood to use as beams near or even within chimneys. An infusion of the bark was fermented to make birdlime to trap wild birds (the practice was described in Mrs Beeton's *Book of Household Management*, 1861). In hard winters, when fodder was short, the upper branches were pollarded to use as sheep and cattle feed.

NAME Medieval monks called it the Holy Tree, probably because of its connections with ancient magic rituals such as decorating houses in midwinter, which were integrated into Christmas celebrations. Its constant evergreen and vital beauty was a symbol of eternal life.

Juniperus communis (Cupressaceae)

JUNIPER

The Combe was ever dark, ancient and dark.
Its mouth is stopped with bramble, thorn, and briar;
And no one scrambles over the sliding chalk
By beech and yew and perishing juniper
Down the half precipices of its sides, with roots
And rabbit holes for steps . . .
  'The Combe', Edward Thomas (1878–1917)

A low-spreading, evergreen bush, juniper is the smallest of Britain's native conifers. Although in the wild it grows on acidic heath, the fact that it tends to the rocky areas betrays juniper's penchant for a light diet of lime. It prefers an open, sunny site, hates being waterlogged and seldom needs pruning. Just how appealing this drought-resistant hardy native can be in a garden is described by Walter de la Mare in his poem 'Trees': 'Of all the trees in England . . . There's none for smell, of bloom and smoke, Like Lime and Juniper . . .' Juniper's narrow, pine-needle-like fine foliage gives it an almost feathery appearance, emphasised by the bright blueish-green of its leaves, contrasted by its reddish-brown bark. Each individual plant is often surprising in its shape: depending on environment, it can be anything from a prostrate, mat-like, scrubby bush to a small, handsome and upright shrub, sometimes sprawling over rocks, or sometimes growing as a small tree. A slightly different form, the low-growing *Juniperus nana*, can be used as ground cover.

ROLE IN LANDSCAPE Juniper is found scattered throughout the British Isles on chalk hills, southern downlands and northern limestone areas, especially upland birch woods. In shallow soils and exposed areas it seldom grows more than a few feet in height, but when conditions are better it becomes a large bush with several straight stems.

GROWTH HABIT Depending on where it is planted, it grows into a low, spreading shrub up to 60cm/24in in height, or an erect tree up to about 10.8m/36ft tall.

PROPAGATION In the wild it is wind-pollinated and the male and female flowers are on separate trees. When stored in cool conditions the seeds retain their vitality for several years. Raising juniper from seed is a slow process, as the seeds must be stratified and kept in shade for eighteen months before sowing. Alternatively, the berries can be sun-dried and sown straight away in a cold frame, but again germination can be slow, up to five years, and then seedlings need to be left for up to two years more before planting out. Propagation from cuttings taken with a heel in late summer or early autumn is a quicker method. Pot in a free-draining mix and keep in a shady cold frame until late the following spring, when they should be planted in a nursery bed. Permanent planting can be carried out in autumn or spring.

TRUNK, BARK AND BRANCHES Reddish bark with multi-coloured wood – pink heartwood and white sapwood in the centre.

LEAVES The sharply pointed, needle-type, linear leaves are borne on young, triangular shoots in whorls of three, 8–20mm/¼–8in long with a central, white band on the green upper surface and grey underneath. These leaves usually stay on the tree for up to three years; even after they are no longer green they remain on the shoots.

BUDS, FLOWERS AND FRUIT The species is unisexual. The small, greenish female flowers – cups of three to eight green scales clustered under the twigs – are small and insignificant. After pollination these expand – by autumn they form a hard, green, berry-like cone which slowly becomes fleshy and bluish-black in colour. The cone-like, yellow male flowers are also small. The female cones gradually ripen in the second or third year, becoming a glaucous blue and finally black. Each fruit contains up to eight angled seeds.

PLANT–ANIMAL RELATIONSHIPS The berries, about the size of currants, are eaten by birds, which swallow them whole and then drop the hard black seeds. Juniper bushes provide year-round cover for thrushes and goldcrests.

HISTORICAL AND OTHER USES Juniper berries impart an agreeably tart flavour to many savoury dishes, and its culinary and medical properties have been exploited for thousands of years. The most famous ancient use was in Egypt as part of a mixture for preserving mummies. The Romans sometimes used juniper berries as a substitute for pepper. They were later used to flavour distilled alcohol (an invention of a son of Henry II of France) and were sought after for marinades for wild boar, venison and pork. Along with caraway seeds they are a traditional ingredient in sauerkraut, are sometimes used in beef or rabbit stews and always with jugged hare. In the Middle Ages, as well as being made into a brown dye, the berries were valued as antiseptics, and the leaves were burnt in public squares and hospitals to counter epidemics. The shoot tips were used to treat whooping cough.

In the sixteenth century the wood was recommended for vine trellises. Thomas Hill, *Most Briefe and Pleasant Treatyse* (1563), wrote that a 'herbar' could be 'framed with Ashen poles, or the Willow . . . if they be made with juniper wode, you need not to repayre nothing therof in ten years after: but if they be made with willow poles, then you must new repayre them in three years after.' It was the plant badge of the Gunn, Macleod, MacNicol, Nicholson, Murray Atholl and Ross clans.

NAME The Latin name *Juniperus* was used by both Virgil and Pliny. The French *genièvre* became the Dutch *genever* from which we get the English word gin, a flavoured spirit first produced in Holland around 1650 and named after the juniper berry which gives it its distinctive flavour. The Swiss city of Geneva was named after its wild junipers.

OTHER SPECIES In the Scottish highlands and on high mountains in the Lake District, the dwarf, prostrate sub-species *nana, Juniperus communis saxatilis*, occurs. The compact, shrubby sub-species *hemisphaerica* is restricted to low cliffs in a few coastal regions. There is also a beautiful little upright tree native to Ireland, the Columnar Irish juniper, which can be seen growing on the Burren in County Mayo; it can be used in garden plantings as an accent tree.

Lavatera arborea (Malvaceae)

TREE MALLOW

. . . There poppies nodding, mock the hope of toil,
There the blue bugloss paints the sterile soil;
Hardy and high, above the slender sheaf,
The slimy mallow waves her silky leaf . . .
'The Village', George Crabbe (1754–1832)

Tree mallow belies its name: it is a biennial shrub, not a tree. A versatile plant, it makes a nice free-standing shrub, hedge or screen, and is particularly eye-catching in herbaceous borders. It likes moist soils but does not like being too wet or cold. It prefers full sun but not extremely hot weather. With its clusters of leaf-covered stems, deep pink and pale purple flowers with dark stripes (similar to hibiscus and holly-hock, to which it is related), it is a cheerful addition to most gardens. Despite its woody stems it behaves like a herbaceous plant, dying back to ground level in winter when it requires mulch for protection. Cutting back old stems stimulates new growth, but this should be delayed until the worst of the frosts are over as new shoots can be damaged in freezing weather. Once established, it is drought-tolerant.

ROLE IN LANDSCAPE Tree mallow grows wild around rocks, cliff bottoms and waste ground near the sea, principally on the south and west coasts as far north as Ayrshire and on the south coast of Ireland, and a little on the east coast on cliff sites in East Lothian. It has been introduced in many places.

GROWTH HABIT Fast-growing biennial, quick to establish but compara-tively short-lived. Up to 3m/10ft maximum in height, usually much shorter.

PROPAGATION Easy to grow from seeds which can be sown directly into a garden bed, germination coming in about fifteen to twenty days. Plant in full sun in fertile, well-drained soil and space plants about 46cm/18in apart. They can also be raised from cuttings or easily grown from the young shoots that grow at the base during the summer. These can be kept in small pots and kept inside over the first winter. Tree mallow often layers itself and a new shrub will grow alongside the parent plant.

TRUNK, BARK AND BRANCHES Erect stems growing to 3m/10ft, woody at the base but the younger stems are soft with stellate hairs, and often very fibrous.

LEAVES Mallow has palm-like furry leaves, shallow with five to seven lobes.

BUDS, FLOWERS AND FRUIT Between May and July mallow produces large, deep pinkish-purple flowers with petals about 14–20cm/5½–8in long. These have a distinctive epicalyx, and are comprised of three segments fused below; the fruit breaks open into several single-seeded nutlets. Sterile cultivars, as with all hybrids in which seed formation is prevented, have longer flowering periods.

PLANT–ANIMAL RELATIONSHIPS Mallow is listed by the Wildlife Trust as one of the best butterfly nectar plants.

HISTORICAL AND OTHER USES Mallow was used in cottage gardens and once also had some medicinal uses; it is still an ingredient in certain herbal cosmetics, hand and face creams.

NAME From Latin *malva*, to soften, referring to its softening or relaxing properties, or to its soft downy leaves.

OTHER SPECIES The smaller tree mallow, also known as the Cornish mallow (*Lavatera cretica*), is an annual or biennial herb 1m/39in in height, or exceptionally 1.5m/5ft. It grows in similar habitats but is more common in the Scilly Isles, the Channel Islands and Cornwall. With its greyish pubescence and dull, lilac-coloured flowers, it resembles the tree mallow but the epicalyx is shorter than the calyx. Various other mallows, such as the musk mallow (*Malva moshata*), the common mallow (*Malva neglecta*) and the dwarf mallow (*Malva sylvestra*), also make interesting garden plants.

Ligustrum vulgare (Oleaceae)

PRIVET

The dawn is smiling on the dew that covers
The tearful roses; lo, the little lovers
That kiss the buds, and all the flutterings
In jasmine bloom, and privet, of white wings,
That go and come, and fly, and peep and hide,
With muffled music, murmured far and wide.
  'The Genesis of Butterflies', Victor Hugo (1802–85)

A tough, branching, semi-evergreen, deciduous shrub which grows rapidly by suckers, privet will grow almost anywhere, ignoring much ill treatment. As it is hardy, thrives on most soils and survives pollution, it was often grown in smoky Victorian cities; although deciduous, it keeps some leaves in winter, especially in towns. But its role in hedging has been superseded by the Japanese privet, *Ligustrum ovalifolium*, while its place in topiary has now been taken over by yew and box. With its dark green leaves and pyramid spikes of white flowers, heavily scented privet makes a robust shrub and can be grown as a single specimen or in a border where it will form dense bushes. It is suited to town gardens and, if uncut, produces flowers that attract butterflies and other insects. It has a wonderful, evocative scent. Like many flowering shrubs, privet is often pruned with little regard to its flowering capacity. It prefers an open, sunny site to flower fully but will grow in semi-shade. As it is drought-resistant and does not accept ground which is very wet, it needs free-draining, preferably alkaline, soil.

GROWTH HABIT Its smooth, dark, wiry stems seldom grow much above 4.5m/15ft.

PROPAGATION Privet is easily raised from seed collected in autumn, stratified, then planted out in late winter and sown in nursery rows before planting out two growing seasons later. New plants can be left in nursery beds for up to four years before permanent planting in the late spring after the last frosts. Hardwood cuttings taken from October to December should be put straight into the ground or into a nursery bed for a year. Privet can also, as it suckers readily, be grown from suckers. Native privet is used as an understock for grafting lilac, to which it is related.

ROLE IN LANDSCAPE Although a tree, privet is mostly found in hedges throughout lowland England and is common in scrub, woodland and downland, often by the sea, and mostly in the south, on fairly fertile, calcareous soils.

TRUNK AND BARK The twigs, which are downy when young, grow into strong, tough, glabrous branches.

LEAVES Small, leathery, short-stalked, narrowly oval leaves develop in March and April, growing darker before falling in winter. Arranged in pairs, each leaf is up to 6cm/2½in long, shiny dark green above and lighter beneath. In hedges the top shoots have leaves in alternating pairs spreading in four directions; the side shoots, because they receive light from only one side, face in just one direction.

BUDS, FLOWERS AND FRUIT Conical clusters of small, bell-shaped white or yellowish, heavily scented flowers appear at the ends of the shoots in June and July, followed by shiny black berries with oily flesh in the autumn, beloved by birds.

PLANT–ANIMAL RELATIONSHIPS When privet hedges and shrubs are untrimmed, bees, butterflies and other insects eagerly work the nectar-rich blossom, attracted by the strong scent. White letter and black hair-streak moths feed on honeydew on the leaves which are susceptible to honey fungus. The leaves are the main food for the caterpillar of the coronet moth and of one of Britain's most ornamental insects, the privet hawk moth. The berries, as Gerard noted, are 'a pleasant meate in winter for owsels, thrushes and divers other birds', particularly the bullfinch.

Privet is also a refuge for hibernating brimstone, small tortoiseshell, comma and peacock butterflies. The leafy bush forms dense thickets, providing excellent cover for nesting birds. If gardeners are not heavy-handed with the trimmer, the bush produces nectar-rich flowers which become nutritious berries, the winter diet of many birds. (The same applies to guelder rose, the wayfaring tree, dogwood and spindle.) Many gardeners grow the Japanese privet (*Ligustrum ovalifolium*) which has broader leaves and is evergreen but offers nothing to English wildlife.

HISTORICAL AND OTHER USES Hard and close-grained, privet, like most members of the olive family, has tough, durable wood. When a sufficient size, it was once made into small tools and was also a source of charcoal. Young twigs were used in basketry and hurdle making. Pink and bluish-green dyes can be obtained from the berries, khaki from the branches and yellow from the leaves. A black dye was also extracted from the fruit, which was used by hatters and glove-makers and also to colour wine and ink. A mild oil from the fruit was once used for lamps and for making soap. An unrelated species, Egyptian privet (*Lawsonia inermis*) produces a henna dye for hair.

NAME *Ligustrum,* from Latin *ligo*, to bind: privet was used by the Romans for tying articles together. The origin of the common name has contradictory sources. One suggestion is that it is from the plant's use in hedges to make gardens 'private'; John Loudon, in the nineteenth century, said the name came from its being 'frequently planted in gardens to conceal privies'.

Lonicera periclymenum (Caprifoliaceae)

HONEYSUCKLE, WOODBINE

As woodbine weds the plant within her reach,
Rough elm or smooth-grained ash, or glossy beech,
In spiral rings ascends the trunk and lays
Her golden tassels on the leafy sprays;
But does a mischief while she lends a grace,
Slackening its growth by such a strict embrace.
    'The Garden', William Cowper (1731–1800)

Honeysuckle, with its distinctive flowers with a long style projecting beyond the funnel-like tube, is one of Britain's most beautiful and most fragrant climbers. No garden should be without it. One of the delights of summer, its pervasive scent is given off in the evening to attract its pollinators, night-flying moths. A scrambling vine, it can be incorporated into a hedge, trained on trelliswork, a pergola or a free-standing support such as an obelisk, grown over an old shrub or tree trunk, or just left to flourish in a reasonably large container near the house where its pervasive evening scent can be enjoyed. It likes full sun but will grow in semi-shade and tolerates most garden soils as long as they are not too dry or too wet, preferring those that are loamy with cool, moist conditions. In open sites the vine can be vigorous and may need pruning to keep it within bounds, both after flowering and again in winter.

Honeysuckle climbs by twining its long woody stem in a clockwise direction around the trunks or stems of stronger supporting plants, or other supports. While it likes to have its roots in the shade, the plant itself reaches up to the sun, so older branches have interesting gnarls and twists. It should not be planted near saplings or other young plants because it will bind tightly, damaging them before they are established. On a trellis, or against a wall, it needs to be kept in check with an annual prune – in woodland the natural competition of trees reduces its vigour. Honey-suckle was trained over arbours in Elizabethan gardens, and the Earl of Lincoln grew it in his London garden, now Lincoln's Inn Fields. In *Much Ado About Nothing*, Shakespeare described 'honeysuckles, ripened by the sun, Forbid the sun to enter . . .' Jane Taylor, *Creative Planting with Climbers,* stresses that the flowers of Britain's native honeysuckle 'are both striking and delectably perfumed, carrying far on the air especially at dusk and dawn', but that many introduced species, the 'most showy honeysuckles, those with the brightest flowers,' often lack scent.

ROLE IN LANDSCAPE Honeysuckle is found in hedgerows, woodlands and scrub, on rocks and cliffs on a wide range of soils throughout England, up to 500m/1,650ft in Teesdale, climbing among dykes, hedges, shrubs and trees. On the Pembrokeshire coast it is a lovely sight. Much of what is seen growing apparently wild, however, is an assortment of alien species that have escaped from gardens.

GROWTH HABIT It can be quite vigorous and, in the right conditions where there is no competition, can climb to 6-10m/ 20–33ft. Although it brightens up parts of suburban London, one gardener said that in her experience it often sulks when planted in urban situations, and becomes prone to mildew, probably because it gets too dry at the roots and does not have enough light.

PROPAGATION It can be raised from seed collected from ripe berries and stratified before sowing in boxes in late winter; the seedlings should be potted up in spring. Unlike many native trees and shrubs, the seeds germinate in the first year after sowing. Hardwood cuttings can be put straight into the ground; semi-hard cuttings taken in late summer need potting up in compost with cane supports before setting out after twelve months in groups of two to three.

TRUNK, BARK AND BRANCHES Its woody stems twine clockwise up plants, reaching a height of 6m/20ft in trees.

LEAVES Ovate, lance-shaped leaves are borne in pairs, each at right angles to the adjacent pairs. Each is 3–7cm/1–2¾in long, dark green above and bluish-green below, smooth-edged and usually pointed. The plant begins to form its leaves in January.

BUDS, FLOWERS AND FRUIT Whorls of small tubular flowers, creamy-white or yellow, each in the shape of a small trumpet, with long styles projecting beyond the funnel-like tube, appear at the end of the stems mainly in early summer and September. Some continue through to September when there can be a second flowering. Flowers, grouped in terminal clusters, are 2.5cm/1in long and 4.5cm across with five sepals, with a widely spread two-lipped mouth with protruding stamens. Flowers change from white to yellow after pollination. Tight heads of fleshy red berries (mildly purgative and not recommended for eating) appear in clusters, each fruit containing up to eight oblong seeds.

PLANT–ANIMAL RELATIONSHIPS
Both its scent and the nectar at the bottom of the flower tube attract pollinating moths; the leaves are food for the larvae of white admiral and marsh fritillary butterflies. With its long tube to the corolla, the flower is adapted to entice the sole insect with a sufficiently long proboscis: the hawk moth, especially the elephant hawk moth, which is its main pollinator. Moths can remove the entire load of pollen in one night, stalked by bats. Bumble bees bite holes at the base to extract the nectar. Once the flowers have turned into berries, robins, thrushes, blue tits, marsh tits, blackcaps, blackbirds, song thrushes and starlings come to feast on the fruit or the seed from dried fruits. Honeysuckle's dense tangled stems make excellent nest sites for many of these visitors. Sometimes squirrels and dormice strip off bits of papery thin bark to weave into their winter nests.

HISTORICAL AND OTHER USES The Elizabethans were the last to use honeysuckle widely in pharmacies, but it is still available as a Bach flower remedy. William Morris incorporated its appearance in several designs, including one of his best-selling fabrics, 'Honeysuckle', in 1874 and later in 'Compton' and 'Woodpecker'. In the 1920s, the great jazz musician Fats Waller recorded one of his best songs, 'Honeysuckle Rose'.

NAME *Lonicera*, after Adam Lonitzer (1528–86), a German physician, botanist and author of a book on natural history. The common name was known from the thirteenth century, presumably a description of the sucking of honey from the long corolla.

Malus sylvestris subsp *sylvestris* (Rosaceae)

CRAB APPLE

Of crab tree blossoms delicate red
He often bends wi' many a wish
O'er the brig rail to view the fish . . .
Each hedge is loaded thick wi' green
And where the hedger late hath been
Tender shoots begin to grow
From the mossy stumps below . . .
  'A Shepherd's Calendar',
  John Clare (1793–1864)

Resistant to cold and tolerant of air pollution, this small, densely branched tree is adaptable and grows into a charming garden plant, the ancient parent of the domestic apple. Its clouds of pretty pink blossoms are a springtime glory, as are its bright, rosy, apple-like fruits in the autumn. With a sturdy trunk, finely formed crown and brown bark it is similar in outline to the cultivated apple, but its fruits are sour. It grows on almost any well-drained soil except damp peat, but prefers an open, sunny position; infertile soils promote root growth at the expense of flowers and fruit. It can be planted in a corner of medium-sized gardens or, in smaller gardens, as a specimen tree. Like other members of the rose family it can be incorporated into a hedge. Indeed, the Royal Society for the Protection of Birds recommends that it is grown as a small hedgerow tree because it flowers and fruits better if pruned, providing more food for birds. Crab apple also improves roadsides, especially grown as an edge species.

ROLE IN LANDSCAPE Like other members of the rose family, notably the dog rose and blackberries, crab apple is usually distinguished by its alternate leaves, prickles, thorns, five-petalled flowers and appealing fruit. Small to medium in height, it is often slightly lop-sided with dense, twisting branches. It is found in ancient woods, especially oak woods, lower hill slopes, hedgerows and scrub on a wide range of soils throughout lowland Britain. Escaped cultivated apple trees are often also found in hedges, but these are usually without thorns and have hairy shoots and leaves with pinker flowers.

GROWTH HABIT It usually grows from a pip into a specimen no taller than 8m/26ft. From its tangled branches come long shoots that extend the crown, short 'spurs' carrying flowers, and sometimes medium-sized shoots ending in a thorn.

PROPAGATION Crab apple is best propagated by extracting seeds from the fruits in winter, then sowing immediately and leaving them undisturbed for a year before lining out 30cm/1ft apart and growing on for a further two years.

TRUNK, BARK AND BRANCHES Its dark grey-brown bark with squarish flakes becomes pale grey, furrowed, cracked and flaky with age. Unlike cultivated apple trees, the shoots often have thorns.

LEAVES The short, pointed leaves which open in late April are ovate, 3–5cm/1–2in long, with a finely toothed margin. They are bright green above and whitish below, and almost hairless.

BUDS, FLOWERS AND FRUIT Clusters of dark pink buds unfurl into pale pink or white five-petalled sweet-scented flowers with yellow anthers, up to just over 3cm/1in across. These are followed by the rounded green fruits on long stalks which ripen to a golden yellow-green and may remain on the tree right through the winter.

PLANT–ANIMAL RELATIONSHIPS Pollinated by bees and other winged insects, crab apple provides shelter for birds and its interweaving branches are used as nesting sites. After the fruits are softened by frosts a wide variety of birds eat them, including blackbirds, robins and mistle thrushes and visiting fieldfares and waxwings; the seeds are eaten by chaffinches and great tits. Red admiral butterflies gorge themselves on the sap from the rotting fruit on the ground below, and the leaves are food for the larvae of figure-of-eight, gothic and pale-shouldered brocade moths.

HISTORICAL AND OTHER USES Crab apple was frequently mentioned by Shakespeare, appearing in *A Midsummer Night's Dream*, *The Tempest* and *Love's Labour Lost* in which the line 'When roasted crabs hiss in the bowl . . .' refers to the fruit which was added to bowls of ale at Christmas. According to Jessica Kerr, *Shakespeare's Flowers*: 'A brew called "Lambswool", consisting of ale, nutmeg, sugar and toasted crab apples, is still served at one of the colleges at Cambridge University . . . It was drunk on the feast day of Lammastide, which falls on 1 August when the apples are ripening.' The sour fruit is made into amber-coloured crab apple jelly or stewed with sugar, syrup or honey. Rich in tannin, which causes the bitterness, crab apple extract was added to tannin-poor wine and mead. The hard, close-grained, red-brown wood was prized for carving, turnery and inlay work, and was once used for bowls, boxes, veneer, saw handles, mallet heads, skittle balls and skittles. The bark produces a dye of varying shades of saffron. Crab apple was the plant badge of the Lamont clan in Scotland.

NAME From Latin *malus*, bad or evil. In his *Herbal* of 1562, Turner stressed that the everyday name varied between crab and scab; another old common name is 'wilding'.

Myrica gale (Myricaceae)

BOG MYRTLE, SWEET GALE

Their groves o' sweet myrtle let foreign lands reckon,
Where bright-beaming summers exalt the perfume;
Far dearer to me yon lone glen o' green breckan,
Wi' the burn stealing under the lang, yellow broom.
  Their groves o' sweet myrtle', Robert Burns (1759–96)

Famed for the strong aromatic scent from its yellow resinous glands and its reddish-brown twigs in winter, this dense shrub is ideal for many gardens, especially for damp areas such as a bog garden, in sunny situations or partial shade. It grows in most soils, especially those that are peaty and slightly acidic. Nitrogen-fixing nodules on the roots enable it to obtain nitrogen from the air so that it flourishes in waterlogged conditions. In a bed with heathers it provides only light shade so other plants can thrive. As it does not regenerate after cutting, its many branches with their shiny, dark green leaves and bright golden-orange catkins should not be pruned. Bog myrtle could well be the plant that inspired William Blake to pen the words, 'To a lovely myrtle bound / Blossoms showering all around . . .'

ROLE IN LANDSCAPE Bog myrtle is abundant in wet moors, fens, healthland and bogs throughout Britain, especially in Scotland (but not in Shetland) and parts of Wales, up to an altitude of 550m/1,800ft. It is less common in drier parts in the east. As it spreads by suckers arising from the roots, it sometimes becomes the dominant plant of boggy areas.

GROWTH HABIT Generally no more than about 1m/39in, occasionally 2m/7ft, rarely reaching its potential of 5m/16½ft tall.

PROPAGATION It can be raised from seed sown in autumn or spring and kept in a cold frame, lined out the following autumn and then grown on for two years before planting out. Seeds, seedlings and young plants must be kept moist at all times. Another method is by layering in spring.

TRUNK, BARK AND BRANCHES It has extremely strong, hard, tortuous, upright branches.

LEAVES Upright branches carry inversely lance-shaped, shiny dark green leaves (paler and usually downy with scattered leaves underneath), which are toothed towards the apex and up to 6cm/2⅜in long.

BUDS, FLOWERS AND FRUIT The stiff, golden-brown catkins open in late March, just before the leaves appear, and continue until May, with male and the smaller female flowers usually borne on separate plants. Catkins appear at the tips of twigs of the previous year's growth. The small, nut-like fruits on the female plants each have two narrow wings to aid wind dispersal, and contain a waxy resin to protect the seed if it falls into water. Tiny seeds form in the female catkins which eventually break up late in the year.

PLANT–ANIMAL RELATIONSHIPS Bog myrtle is visited by insects including small flies and is the foodplant of the beautiful brocade, great brocade, dotted clay and rosy marsh moths. Birds consider these moths a tasty dish, so they also make frequent visits.

HISTORICAL AND OTHER USES It is used in moth-balls, as a repellent for midges and as a substitute for hops in home brewing. In some parts of Scotland, it was a symbol of love. It was the plant badge of five clans: the Campbells, Campbells of Cawdor, MacAlpines, MacIntyres and MacIvers/MacIvors.

NAME From Greek *myrike*, a shrub, supposedly tamarisk. In 1597 Gerard called it the Dutch myrtle tree and wilde myrtle, a translation of the German *Mirtlebaum*, given because it was considered to be a kind of myrtle. The common name is from Old English *gagel*, found in place names such as Galsworthy.

Pinus sylvestris (Pinaceae)

SCOTS PINE

This is the forest primeval.
The murmuring pines and
*   the hemlocks . . .*
Stand like Druids of old . . .
*   'Evangeline', Henry Wadsworth*
*   Longfellow (1807–92)*

Scots pine, along with juniper and yew, is one of Britain's three native conifers. A familiar and picturesque tree, grown both for its timber and for its beauty, it is distinguished from other pines by its umbrella-shape, blue-green foliage and scaly branches. Like all cone-bearing and resinous trees, it suits cold and elevated areas, where the soil is thin, poor or sandy. Because it adapts to harsh conditions (apart from sea winds or high rainfall), Scots pine is often said to grow almost anywhere. It does, though, have preferences to be free-standing in light or sandy soils at low or moderate elevation and to have full sun, moist soil and a northern exposure. With its rusty-red or red-orange bark, it looks splendid in many large gardens or parks, even cities. An urban study completed in 2002 rated ash, larch and Scots pine as among Britain's top pollution-busters, the most efficient trees absorbing lethal fumes from the atmosphere.

ROLE IN LANDSCAPE Long ago, Scots pine made up most of the ancient Caledonian Forest, remnants of which survive in Deeside, the Cairngorms, Rannock Moor and Wester Ross. During the felling of the eighteenth and nineteenth centuries, one of the oldest trees, the 'Granny Afric', was spared solely because the nearby river was too shallow to transport floating logs. Since being re-introduced from Scotland to southern England in 1660, Scots pine has re-established itself as a commercial tree, despite the introduction of foreign fast-growing firs and exotic conifers.

Scots pine, with its bottle-green shortish needles, and red tinge to the boughs, is genetically different from similar long-needled European varieties and shows distinct features. Over thousands of years, small variations have made it develop individual characteristics. Corsican pine, for example, has longer needles and a grey, rather reddish bark. When mature, the top of a Scots pine tree is often more like that of a beech or an oak in outline than the usual habit of pines. How light affects its dramatic shape can be seen by comparing Scots pines planted as timber crops in regimented forests with those that are self-sown in woods.

GROWTH HABIT Occasionally reaching 40–50m/140–170ft, it lives to 400 years or more.

PROPAGATION Once collected, seed stores better underground rather than in packets. Some say that seeds should be planted soon after they fall out of the cones; others that they should be chilled for up to ten weeks before sowing in well-pulverised soil of a rather dry, sandy nature – and that this should be done in about the middle of April in England, and the first week in May in Scotland. William Ablett, *English Trees and Tree-Planting* (1880), gives yet another method: 'If only a comparatively small quantity of seed is needed, the seed can be obtained by merely exposing the cones to the sunshine in any sunny situation sloping to the south, when in a few days' time they will open, and the seeds can be sifted out. After the seeds have been collected, they should be moistened with water which will detach them from the kind of chaff that covers them, after which they are made clean by sifting.' He added that they were ready for transplanting when about two years old.

TRUNK, BARK AND BRANCHES The bark on mature trees is dark reddish-brown, and tinged with yellow or pink towards the top of the tree where it becomes smoother, contrasting with the lower bark which is a more rugged dark brown. Bark is fissured into elongated plates.

LEAVES The slender, bluish-green needles are 5–7cm/2–3in long, set in scaly sheaths in pairs, often with a spiral twist.

BUDS, FLOWERS AND FRUIT The small female cones are pinkish with scales open to receive the pollen shed by the male cones in May. The smaller male cones are usually yellow, though they can be red, densely clustered around the lower parts of the new shoots. There is a gap of a year between fertilisation and the time the cone takes to become brown, woody and seed-bearing – the scales open so that the winged seeds can fly into the air.

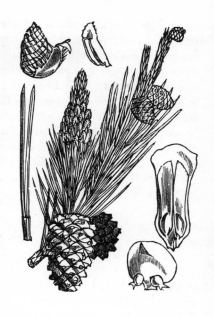

PLANT–ANIMAL RELATIONSHIPS

Red squirrels extract and devour the seed from the cones while they are still on the trees, before they are eaten by crossbills or drop to the ground and are consumed by other animals, including mice, voles and the rare Scottish crossbill (*Loxia scotica*). Black grouse and capercaille eat the buds and shoots. Among the many birds associated with this ancient tree are common insect- or seed-eating birds such as the chaffinch, siskin, crested tit, crossbill, tree creeper and woodpecker, as well as large raptors such as the golden eagle. The caterpillars of the pine looper moth eat the needles, and various other insects live between the flakes of the bark – these in turn provide food for birds. The decrease in red squirrel numbers is due not only to the continuing spread of the introduced American grey but also because it cannot breed unless it has a suitable place (preferably a Scots pine) in which to build or refurbish its 'drey' – a small, ball-shaped structure high up on a branch close to the trunk, made from twigs and sticks and lined with soft material.

HISTORICAL AND OTHER USES

Because of its height and strength, Scots pine was considered the king of the forest. It was planted on the graves of Scottish warriors who died in battle, and is the traditional emblem of the MacGregor clan. A strong general purpose timber known as deal or redwood, Scots pine was used in boat and ship building, both in the structure and for masts. In contrast to box wood which sinks, Scots pine is extremely buoyant, as are the ropes which were made from its roots, beaten into threads and spun like hemp. The wood is still used for house joists, planks, roof timbers and telegraph poles; the wood of younger trees was sold as pit timber to prop up mine tunnels, and for palings, staves and building laths. The hardest and best quality wood is usually from trees grown upon poor soils at great altitudes. The abundant resin was turned into an ingredient to add to paint and varnish and was also made into pitch to make surfaces more waterproof, especially when sealing the hulls of boats or the joints in roofs. Christmas trees of young Scots pine have become a by-product of heathland management and conservation. In places like Ashdown Forest in Sussex, any naturalised, invasive Scots pine is removed and sold in December.

NAME Latin *Pinus*, pine tree; *sylvestris*, of the forest.

Populus nigra (Salicaceae)

BLACK POPLAR

The poplars are fell'd; farewell to the shade,
And the whispering sound of the cool colonnade!
The winds play no longer and sing in the leaves,
Nor Ouse on his bosom their image receives.
   'The Poplar Field', William Cowper (1731–1800)

With its immensely tall, slender trunk of often gnarled black bark, and its upward-pointing branches that bear scarlet catkins, black poplar is one of Britain's most distinctive native trees – and the most endangered. Exposed sites, parks and large gardens are especially suitable for black poplar, and it grows rapidly in wetland regions, but due to its height and long roots it should not be planted near buildings or where there are drains. Like other poplars, it often grows in soils where oak, ash or pine do not flourish. It is best planted in a damp place, on fertile soil in a well-sheltered site with male and female trees in close proximity to enable pollination. Oliver Rackham, an authority on the history of the English landscape, considers that black poplar, more than any other tree, 'reminds us of the splendour of the medieval countryside'. Alas, most planted poplars in Britain are now hybrids of *P. nigra* and foreign species.

GROWTH HABIT Fast-growing, it reaches about 30m/98ft.

PROPAGATION Not all seeds are fertile. It does not sucker, so hardwood cuttings 20–25cm/8–10in long are often taken; in the wild, like the willow, black poplar often regenerates from fallen trees, branches or damaged roots which take root. Cuttings are more likely to sprout if grown in cultivated soil with the top end level with the soil surface.

ROLE IN LANDSCAPE The black poplar, identified by its black bark, height, obvious leaning stance and compact crown, grows in wet woods and stream sides, happily surviving occasional flooding. It was once seen across large areas of southern, eastern and central England west to Cheshire. Numbers have declined dramatically over the last century and it is now very rare. Most trees are found south of a line from the Mersey to the Humber estuaries, with a few scattered individuals occurring as far north as the Tees. The greatest concentration is in the Aylesbury Vale, which holds approximately half of the British population, with a few hundred along the River Severn and in Somerset, Suffolk and Shropshire.

The black poplars of many of John Constable's Suffolk paintings, including *The Hay Wain* (1821), depicting Flatford on the Stour, exist no more. Most of the old remaining trees are coming to the end of their lives. In Cheshire the black poplar survives at the north-western limit of its range, but the old, scattered trees are no longer regenerating naturally. As a wetland tree, black poplar has been badly affected by land drainage. In 1982, the national number was estimated at fewer than 7,000 of which there are fewer than 100 clones; there were only about 200 female trees, not many growing near males, so sexual regeneration was poor. As a result, the black poplar became part of a Wildlife Trust Action Plan, and the Corporation of London introduced it to Highgate Wood, Hampstead Heath and Queen's Park in Kilburn.

TRUNK, BARK AND BRANCHES The tree has down-sweeping branches and up-sweeping twigs. While the bark is thickened, rugged and furrowed on older trees, dark-grey to black, it is thin and grey-green on young trees. Irregular cracks and fissures depend on the age of the tree. It sheds its branches, something that gardeners need to remember.

LEAVES The deep green leaves appear in April and May, roughly triangular or diamond-shaped, and slightly serrated with small teeth. They are about 5–7cm/2–2¾in long, becoming yellow in autumn.

BUDS, FLOWERS AND FRUIT Male and female flowers are borne on 3–5cm/1–2in long catkins on separate trees. The male flowers are very red with red anthers, while female flowers have green stigmas and masses of white fluff.

PLANT–ANIMAL RELATIONSHIPS The tree is host to many birds and herbivorous insects, some of which live in the thick, fissured bark, including *Byctiscus populi,* an attractive, metallic green or coppery leaf-rolling weevil normally associated with aspen.

HISTORICAL AND OTHER USES Not as durable as ash or oak, black poplar is used to make plywood and veneers, or as a softwood substitute in pallets and pulp. Once, however, because of its fire resistance and shock-absorbing qualities, it was prized by tool and weapon makers, and was used to make wagon bottoms, stable partitions, rifle butts, buffers on early railway carriages and flooring near fireplaces. Coppiced timber was used in baskets, stakes, scaffold poles and rafters. A black poplar in Portsmouth is a descendant of the tree from which the arrows for the armoury of the warship *Mary Rose* were made. Gerard wrote of an ointment made from its buds and said it was 'very well knowne to the Apothecaries'.

NAME Latin *Populus*, poplar; *nigra*, black, referring to the bark.

Populus tremula (Salicaceae)

ASPEN

All day and all night, save winter, every weather,
Above the inn, the smithy, and the shop,
The aspens at the cross-roads talk together
Of rain, until their last leaves fall from the top.
Out of the blacksmith's cavern comes the ringing
Of hammer, shoe, and anvil; out of the inn
The clink, the hum, the roar, the random singing –
The sounds that for these fifty years have been.
The whisper of the aspens is not drowned,
And over lightless pane and footless road,
Empty as sky, with every other sound
Not ceasing, calls their ghosts from their abode . . .
    'Aspens', Edward Thomas (1878–1917)

With its air of elegance – it is tall in proportion to its girth – and the sound of the constant movement of its leaves, the aspen can be spectacular. It thrives in moist sites, particularly low-lying land near rivers or estuaries or inland bogs – even on mountain ledges, but never in dry areas. It should not be planted near drains, as its roots will seek the water in them. Its grey-green appearance makes an interesting contrast with the deeper shades of green of other garden plants. Caution: it is spreading in habit and has a tendency to sucker, so in gardens it needs regular pruning or coppicing.

GROWTH HABIT Aspen grows just under a metre a year in the first ten years, then slows down. When mature at about 50 years it can be as tall as 15–20m/50–70ft. The tallest aspen in Britain, in Ardgay, Sutherland, is 20m/70ft, and a staggering 90cm/36in in girth. Usually they are much smaller, often forming suckering thickets of one sex in the wild.

PROPAGATION In the wild aspen often spreads by suckering or by airborne seed. Fresh seeds germinate quickly but do not keep their vigour long. William Robinson said that Britain's native poplars were 'among the hardiest of trees and the easiest to increase and grow', but this is not always so easy with aspen.

ROLE IN LANDSCAPE Hardy and fast-growing, adaptable to a wide range of soils and conditions, aspen is found throughout the British Isles, in woodlands, hedgerows and parks. It is more frequent in the north by streams and in damp places. The large aspen stands in the Scottish Highlands are unique, a remnant of the boreal woodlands that colonised the area after the last glaciation. The trembling and whispering of the leaves have inspired writers and poets. 'How I shake . . . In very truth do I, as 'twere an aspen leaf' (Shakespeare, *Henry IV Part II*, 2: 4);

'Those aspen leaves of theirs never leave wagging' (Thomas Moore). John Clare referred to 'the brustling noise, that oft deceives'. Gerard Manley Hopkins lamented the felling of 'My aspens dear, whose airy cages quelled, Quelled or quenched in leaves the leaping sun.'

TRUNK, BARK AND BRANCHES Its bole is covered with smooth grey bark.

LEAVES The rustling sound is caused by the vertically flattened leaf-stalks which are exceptionally long. The leaves themselves are rather nondescript in shape – broad, tending to circular, with sinuous margins and a blunt apex.

BUDS, FLOWERS AND FRUIT Catkins bloom during March and April.

PLANT–ANIMAL RELATIONSHIPS Many animals eat the leaves, especially those on the suckers surrounding a tree. Insects, including caterpillars of the chevron, large dark prominent, scarce chocolate-tip and twin-spotted quaker moth, appear from May onwards. Aspen is well known for attracting *Byctiscus populi*, a handsome, metallic green or coppery leaf-rolling weevil, which is eaten by birds. Aspen was the staple food of the beaver in Scotland before its extinction. Some of the dead wood should be left, as this also supports insects. Aspen stands in Scottish woods have a diverse insect community with rare species, including seven listed in the Red Data Book (a standard list of conservation status, especially of rare and endangered species); their importance has recently been recognised by the Council of Europe.

HISTORICAL AND OTHER USES The wood, like that of other poplars, is of poor quality, but it was once made into matches, clogs, floorboards, pulp and other objects. Branches were used at funerals and wakes; the ancient Greeks believed that aspen grew in the Underworld. It is one of the many species of tree whose wood, at some stage, has been claimed for Christ's cross; in Russia it was known as the tree of Judas.

NAME Latin *Populus tremula*, trembling poplar, because its leaves shake constantly in the wind. The common name is from Old English *æsp*; the introduction of the current form was noted by Gerard in 1597: 'In English Aspe, and Aspen tree'.

Potentilla fruticosa (Rosaceae)

SHRUBBY CINQUEFOIL

Here's fine rosemary, sage and thyme . . .
Here's balm and hissop, and cinquefoil,
All fine herbs, it is well known.
Let none despise the merry, merry cries
Of famous London-town!
  'The Cries of London', anon.,
  seventeenth century

A deciduous, multi-stemmed, small, bushy shrub with a low spreading habit, it displays clear yellow buttercup-like flowers in abundance over a long period from late spring to mid-autumn. Versatile and long-flowering, shrubby cinquefoil suits most gardens, is low-maintenance and can be useful in borders, rock or gravel areas in water gardens, or in a low hedge. It flourishes where rainfall is dependable, as its thin woody roots are shallow to moderately deep. Growing best in open situations with plenty of sun, it needs full sun in order to flower well, and a light, free-draining soil but it is tolerant of a wide range of soils. In the eighteenth century, Philip Miller wrote that shrubby cinquefoil was 'commonly culti-vated in the Nursery Gardens as a flowering Shrub'. Fashions change: now it is sometimes included among shrubs regarded as weeds, as it can spread rapidly by producing a profuse number of suckers.

GROWTH HABIT Whether it occurs as a low mat or as an erect shrub, its twiggy stems seldom exceed 1m/39in, reaching a maximum of 1.5m/5ft. Spring pruning of the older shoots keeps it more compact.

PROPAGATION In the wild, shrubby cinquefoil regenerates both from wind-dispersed seed and from suckers. Cuttings of late summer shoots, 10–12cm/4–4¾in long, can be potted in sandy compost in a propagator, under polythene, or in a cold greenhouse.

ROLE IN LANDSCAPE Shrubby cinquefoil is rare in the wild and found only in two upland areas in northern England, mostly on rock ledges and at the margins of lakes and river. Although it grows throughout the northern hemisphere, including Ireland, most plants are escapes from garden cultivars. Its range has diminished since it was first recorded on the banks of the Tees in Yorkshire by the English botanist, John Ray, *Historica Plantarum* (1688).

TRUNK, BARK AND BRANCHES The bark is dark brown or purplish and peeling, the trunk strong and the twiggy stems hairy.

LEAVES Dark green, alternate, 4cm/1½in long, composed of three to seven narrow, oblong leaflets.

BUDS, FLOWERS AND FRUIT The yellow, saucer-shaped flowers with a prominent centre appear in late May or June until late September, singly or in groups, with male and female flowers (difficult to distinguish from one another) always carried on separate plants. The females produce single-seeded fruits in a clustered head.

PLANT–ANIMAL RELATIONSHIPS The flower is visited by insects including picture-winged flies. Deer are supposed to dislike it.

NAME Latin *Potentilla* from *potens*, power, because the plant was believed to guard against witches and drive out fevers; *fruticosa*, shrubby.

Prunus avium (Rosaceae)

WILD CHERRY, GEAN

Loveliest of trees, the cherry now
Is hung with bloom along the bough,
And stands about the woodland ride
Wearing white for Eastertide.
  'A Shropshire Lad',
  A. E. Housman (1859–1936)

Wild cherry is one of Britain's most attractive native deciduous trees. With its straight trunk, crown of spreading branches and clusters of white blossom in spring followed by sprays of large flowers on longish stems, and eventually dark red cherries in August, it gives constant delight. It can be planted in gardens of all sizes and tolerates light shade, but prefers full sun. It requires moist, well-drained soil, preferably neutral to alkaline, and does better in richer sites that are not too wet. As it does not cast heavy shade, many plants can grow beneath it, but it is prone to surface rooting so should not be planted where the roots might cause problems, such as in lawns or beside paths and paving.

GROWTH HABIT This, the original cherry, forerunner of all cultivated varieties, grows to about 7.5m/25ft in height, often less.

PROPAGATION Seed can be gathered at the same time as the birds arrive to feed on the fruit. With the flesh removed, the stones should be stored in moist sand until the following spring when they can be sown in nursery beds. Thin out as necessary and plant in permanent position when four to five years old.

ROLE IN LANDSCAPE Fairly common throughout Britain in or around the edges of open broad-leaved woodland, wild cherry is also found in lowland woods, often in the understorey layer of oak woods. It likes fertile, often base-rich, soil, thriving in chalk, limestone-based soil or clay overlying chalk. It is planted along roadsides, but not in very exposed areas or close to the coast.

TRUNK, BARK AND BRANCHES The smooth bark is a lovely reddish-brown, banded with rough, orangey-brown breathing pores. In older specimens it sometimes peels in horizontal strips. The greyish-brown twigs have alternate russet-brown buds which in April and May release long-stalked, slightly drooping, leaves.

LEAVES The ovate to elliptical leaves are 15cm/6in long with toothed margins and downy below. In autumn they turn bronze and can change to shades of yellow, orange and red-brown.

BUDS, FLOWERS AND FRUIT The fragrant clusters of white flowers are hermaphrodite (having both male and female organs), bloom from April to May, and are pollinated by bees. As they are self-sterile, to ensure there is a crop two or more trees must be planted. Each flower has two to six, cup-shaped, five-petalled flowers on long, grooved stalks. These appear as the leaves unfurl, often covering the crown in blossoms before the leaves are fully open. The small, shiny fruits, up to 1.2cm/½in across, ripen in July and August, changing colour from yellow and bright red to dark purplish-red, almost black. These are edible but taste bittersweet, and birds often get them before humans.

PLANT–ANIMAL RELATIONSHIPS Pollinating bees and other insects, including butterflies, flock to the nectar. The shiny cherries which appear in autumn are larger than most British wild fruits, above the upper size limit for smaller birds. Robins cannot eat them, but they are enjoyed by woodpigeons and starlings. The leaves are eaten by forest bugs including a large shield-bug, by the caterpillars of several moths, by foxes and badgers. They are galled by the same fungus that causes peach-leaf curl.

HISTORICAL AND OTHER USES Heavy, hard and tough, cherry wood is sought after by cabinetmakers and craftsmen for panelling, joinery, veneers, furniture, turned bowls, pipes, musical instruments and wood sculpture.

NAME The common name is from Old French *cherise*; the north country version, gean, from modern French *guigne*, sweet cherry.

Prunus padus (Rosacea)

BIRD CHERRY

The cherry trees bend over and are shedding
On the old road where all that pass are dead,
Their petals, strewing the grass as for a wedding
This early May morn when there is none to wed.
    'The Cherry Trees', Edward Thomas (1878–1917)

Bird cherry is at its best in early summer, when its clusters of small white flowers perfume the air with a scent reminiscent of vanilla and almonds. With its rounded crown and steeply ascending upper branches, it is suitable for gardens of all sizes; it prefers an open site and damp soil, and can be grown alone or incorporated in a hedge. It sends up shoots with smooth, dark brown bark, making it pleasing in winter months. As it casts only light shade, it allows plants to grow underneath. Despite being hardy, it does not like exposure to strong winds, especially salt-laden coastal winds.

ROLE IN LANDSCAPE Normally found with other trees as part of the understorey in pockets of old woodland near streams, it grows in moist, deciduous, oak and birch woodland and in scrub. It has a northern distribution and is found in most parts of Scotland except the far north, and throughout northern England, and up to 500m/1,650ft in North Yorkshire. South of its line of natural distribution, it has been planted.

GROWTH HABIT Shrub-like in stature, usually around 3m/10ft high and seldom reaching its potential of 15m/50ft, it often qualifies as a shrub rather than a tree.

PROPAGATION Fruits collected in July should be stored, with the flesh removed, until the following spring before sowing, thinning and planting out in the same way as wild cherry.

TRUNK, BARK AND BRANCHES The bark is glossy and dark reddish-brown with a strong pleasant smell of bitter almonds. It has short horizontal bands of orange breathing pores.

LEAVES The leathery, elliptical, finely toothed leaves, dull green above, pale green below and up to 10cm/4in long, unfold in May. They turn gold and red before falling in October.

BUDS, FLOWERS AND FRUIT Long spikes of loose, hanging racemes with up to about forty white, five-petalled, almond-scented, self-fertile flowers. These become spherical, sour, shiny black fruits ripening in late summer, ranging in colour from yellow to dark brown.

PLANT–ANIMAL RELATIONSHIPS The flowers attract many pollinating bees and flies and the leaves are host to numerous insects. The small black fruits, resembling miniature cherries, are full of tannin and inedible to humans, but birds love them as they are much smaller than those of the wild cherry – they are eaten by thrushes, followed by robins, warblers and hawfinches. Geoffrey Smith, one of the original panellists on BBC's *Gardeners' Question Time*, wrote in *The Joy of Wildlife Gardening*: '"Bird cherry" is well named, for its fruits are to blackbirds what green figs are to me; utterly irresistible! . . . The black fruits are, of course, devoured as they ripen . . .' The fragrant flower sprays are visited by bees, hoverflies and butterflies, and are also consumed by bullfinches. Caterpillars of various species feed on the foliage, including the small ermine moth whose communal tents may be both numerous and conspicuous. But the leaves are poisonous to domestic animals, especially goats.

HISTORICAL AND OTHER USES Smokers' pipes were made from bird cherry, and the timber of light sapwood and darker brown heartwood is still used for cabinet making.

NAME The common name was recorded in 1597 by Gerard as 'The Birds Cherry-tree'.

Prunus spinosa (Rosaceae)

BLACKTHORN, SLOE

A Trie than I sie than
Of Cherries on the Braes;
Belaw to I saw to
Ane Buss of bitter Slaes.
　　　'The Cherrie and the Slae', Alexander Montgomerie (c.1545–c.1611)

The blackthorn, more of an upright shrub than a tree, is ideal for small gardens if controlled. In many situations, however, it suits larger gardens only because of its spreading and suckering habit. A densely spiked bush, with very dark, almost black, bark and large sharp spines along the branches, it is particularly noticeable for its sheets of white blossom on bare twigs and its bright, small, plum-like fruits, called sloes, which mature in October. Its advantages are many: it keeps its green leaves until October or November, it gives a display of spring blossom earlier than the hawthorn, its fruits are edible, and it has a compact, spiny form. Its tough thorny growth makes an impenetrable hedge for birds to nest in, and can also serve as a first-class barrier to intruders, both human and animal. Smaller plants growing beneath it are also protected. William Robinson wrote: 'What is more beautiful in the landscape than a snowy wreath of old sloe trees in spring, seen beyond the wide fields, or more delicate in bud when seen at hand?' Blackthorn can withstand exposure to strong winds, is generally hardy and, as long it is not permanently wet, tolerant of almost any soil except the most peaty and acid. It tolerates some shade as long as it is not too heavy. As the blossoms often appear in March during the period of cold east winds, a 'blackthorn winter' is an old country name for any cold spell that occurs around this time.

GROWTH HABIT Seldom reaches more than 4m/13ft in height, but sometimes takes the form of a small tree up to 6m/20ft tall.

PROPAGATION Although blackthorn is propagated both in the wild and in gardens by seed, it is also free-suckering. In the autumn, birds eat the flesh of the sloes, and drop the indigestible seeds. Gardeners who want to propagate blackthorn usually use the same method as for wild cherry; seedlings can be planted out after three years.

ROLE IN LANDSCAPE Where there is sufficient light, it is common in the understorey in old broadleaved woods, on woodland margins and in scrub and hedgerows on most soils except the most acid.

TRUNK, BARK AND BRANCHES The spine-tipped branchlets protect the young foliage from browsing animals. On older plants the bark fractures into small, scale-like squares.

LEAVES Small, oval, finely toothed, fresh green leaves appear on reddish stalks in spring after the flowers; as they mature become longer, up to 4cm/1½in, narrower and a darker, duller green.

BUDS, FLOWERS AND FRUIT The little white flowers, each with five petals and red anthers, blossom in March and April, appearing before the leaves on short lateral spine-tipped branchlets. The dark tangle of spiny branches smothered with a mass of tiny, pure-white flowers is one of the joys of spring in the countryside. Autumn is also a high point when lustrous, round, bluish-black sloes glow among the foliage. These will only form where there is no danger of late frosts that might kill the flowers. Like the cherry fruit, the sloe is a drupe or stone fruit: the outer part is fleshy, the inner part hard and stony, containing a single seed. Damsons and most other forms of garden plums are derived from forms of this native plant. Sloe flesh is mouth-witheringly acid – far too tart to eat – but when infused with sugar in gin or vodka and stored for a while, it makes a delicious drink.

PLANT–ANIMAL RELATIONSHIPS A blackthorn hedge makes an excellent, well-protected nesting site for birds. Chaffinches, greenfinches and dunnocks prefer blackthorn and hawthorn to any other species for nesting. In years when there is an abundance of fruit, birds eat large amounts, usually after the winter frosts have softened it. The flowers produce nectar for humble bees and early-flying small tortoiseshell butterflies. The leaves are the main foodplant of the brown and black hairstreak butterflies, the latter being a highly restricted species in England, occurring only in the woodlands of the East Midlands and on dense stands of blackthorn on heavy clay soils between Oxford and Peterborough. It is unlikely that growing blackthorn in gardens, even in large groups, would attract such a rare butterfly. The bush's most numerous visitors are night-flying moths, including the chinese character, the common quaker, the twin-spotted quaker, the vapourer, the winter and the yellow-tail. It is also host to a gall midge which may produce up to sixty blisters round the margin of a single leaf.

HISTORICAL AND OTHER USES Sloe stones have been found in abundance by archaeologists at Neolithic sites — nearly a wheelbarrow-full near Glastonbury. It is not known if the sloes were used for dyeing or valued because of their astringency. Later records show that all parts of the plant were brewed up by herbalists, and the leaves dried to make an infusion. For sloe gin or vodka, take sloes picked in autumn (they are best after the first frost), prick them, pack them in bottles with plenty of sugar and cover with the spirit. They should be sealed for at least a few months, but the flavour improves if the drink is matured for a couple of years. Large producers now import pulped sloes from Eastern Europe. Sloes also make jam and jelly, and can be used instead of juniper berries to flavour pork. The berries release a dye that was used in marking-ink. Knobbly walking sticks, the teeth in wooden garden rakes and marquetry were made from the hard, durable wood. The first golf clubs in Scotland were made from Scottish ash (the wood of spears), glued and bound on to sticks of local blackthorn, used to hit balls made of leather stuffed with feathers. Buckthorn was the plant badge for the MacQuarrie clan.

NAME Old English *blaec-thorn*, referring to its blackish bark.

Quercus robur (Fagaceae)

PEDUNCULATE OAK

He that hath seen a great Oak dry and dead,
Yet clad with relics of some Trophies old,
Lifting to heaven her aged hoary head,
Whose foot in ground hath left but feeble hold . . .
And though she owe her fall to the frost wind,
Yet of the devout people is adored,
And many young plants spring out of her rind:
That such this City's honour was of yore,
And 'mongst all cities flourished much ore.
    'The Ruins of Rome', Edmund Spenser (1552–99)

Native throughout Europe, *Quercus robur* runs like a golden thread through the history of these islands from Druid times. With its massive frame and broad, dome-shaped silhouette, it is Britain's most distinguished tree and the most important forest tree in England. It is excellent as a large feature tree or, being tolerant of moderate cutting back and occasional pollarding or coppicing, as a specimen tree for a smaller garden or as a hedge. Young oaks keep their leaves during winter, so add muted colours to hedges. Michael Chinery, the well known naturalist, writes in *The Living Garden:* 'Even if you have room to plant an oak you wouldn't be around to see it in its full glory. But this needn't stop you from planting a sapling. Regular pruning will keep it in check and you can have a fine oak bush in less than ten years.' As stressed elsewhere in this book, pruning also inhibits root growth. Oak grows in sun or semi-shade and likes deep, fertile soils, tolerating those that are damp but not waterlogged. Although reasonably drought-tolerant it does not thrive on dry, shallow soils and dislikes salty winds in coastal sites.

GROWTH HABIT When grown on rich soil in sheltered valleys, oak becomes a tall tree, with a straight trunk, up to around 40m/131ft with a tall, irregular, open crown. But it is more often lower and with a widely spaced, domed crown; in exposed situations in unfavourable conditions, it becomes dwarf and bushy. Odd though the comparison is, oak and primroses are frequently seen in companionship.

PROPAGATION The seed germinates freely and propagation is solely from acorns, which are best collected ripe as they fall to the ground, and then sown immediately in beds protected from mice with a deep layer of soil over a sawdust marking layer. One advantage of collecting acorns from local trees is that they have a known provenance. Seedlings should be planted out after one year and replanted every second year until 75cm/30in tall, when they can be planted in their permanent position. During 2002, to celebrate the Queen's Golden Jubilee, a sapling grown from an acorn collected from a gnarled 800-year-old oak in Windsor Great Park was planted in Victoria Embankment Gardens, London. The provenance of most oaks, though, is unknown. Of the estimated 80 million broadleaved trees and shrubs planted annually in Britain, around 56 million are from the continent; British nurseries import up to an estimated 30 tonnes of Dutch acorns annually.

ROLE IN LANDSCAPE The sturdy, majestic English oak with its air of grandeur is the tree that most readily evokes English history and a vanishing landscape. It is also often regarded as a national tree, symbolic of steadfastness, massiveness and strength. Of the 300 or so species of oak recognised in the world only two are native to Britain. They can reach 1,500 years of age – compare this with poplars and hornbeams, which in normal circumstances do not live for more than a few centuries (though longer if pollarded). With its immense, spreading branches carrying round-lobed leaves, oak was considered sacred by the ancient Greeks and Romans, as well as by the Gauls and Britons. Druids acted out their ceremonies beneath its spreading branches, cutting mistletoe from its trunk for one of their most sacred rites.

Pedunculate oak is found in woodland, open ground and, when pollarded, in hedgerows throughout England on heavy clays and loams, especially on neutral or lime-rich soils, up to around 300m/985ft. Where the soil is suitably deep and rich, it is dominant in lowland woods. The most famous ancient oak in England still standing is a tourist attraction in Sherwood Forest, Nottinghamshire, and is said to have had associations with Robin Hood in the early fourteenth century when he was poaching the King's deer to help the poor. This venerable but hollow old tree, now supported, has a girth of nearly 10.6m/35ft. Britain's oldest oak is at Bowthorpe Park Farm, near Witham on the Hill, Lincolnshire. The Winfarthing oak in Norfolk was described as old in the reign of William the Conqueror in the late eleventh century; it was still standing in 1820. Old trees possess amazing vitality. Even after the core has decayed, leaving just a husk of timber, many continue to produce leaves and acorns. The most worrying threat to the oak population is the appearance in England of 'sudden oak death', caused by a European fungus, *Phytophthora ramorum*, which arrived as a twig and foliage infection in rhododendrons and other shrubs. Its spread is at present limited, but it is an ominous introduction as it has caused serious mortality in oaks and other species in North America.

TRUNK, BARK AND BRANCHES The trunk is grey-brown, smooth at first then becoming rough and fissured. Large branches grow low on the tree, often spreading almost horizontally.

LEAVES Oak's instantly recognisable, pale green, deeply lobed, short-stalked or stalkless ovate leaves, widest above the middle, have three to six

rounded lobes each side tapering to two small ear-like lobes at the base. They vary in size, up to about 14cm/5½in long, sometimes bronze or brown when they unfurl in May; the second, summer, growth can be tinged with red.

BUDS, FLOWERS AND FRUIT
Pale-green flowers of both sexes appear at the same time as the leaves, the males in slender, hanging catkins 3–8cm/1–3in long and the females in stalked spikes at the tips of shoots. The latter are followed by acorns, looking like tiny, shiny eggs sitting in a rough-textured cup. Held singly or in clusters of two to three on long stalks, they are green at first but turn brown when ripe in autumn when they drop to the ground.

PLANT–ANIMAL RELATIONSHIPS This 'host of hosts' is the most important of all Britain's native trees as a habitat for wildlife – almost a complete ecosystem in its own right. It attracts a rich variety of 284 insect species, including caterpillars which provide food for birds. It also acts as a landmark for colonies of one of Britain's rarest butterflies, the purple emperor, while the larvae of purple hairstreak butterflies are among the dozens of different butterfly and moth caterpillars that feed on the young leaves. The moths include the maiden's blush, the oak , and the green oak-roller which lowers itself from the branches on a long silken thread. More than thirty species of gall wasps occur on oak – each species lays its eggs in the roots, bark, buds, leaves, catkins or acorns. Wasp grubs secrete chemicals that trigger the plant to produce gall tissues to enclose them, but they do not cause serious damage – it is part of the ecology of the tree, even when it results in misshapen acorns.

Oak also attracts lichens, fungi, bats, squirrels, voles, wood mice, spiders, beetles and a huge variety of birds including warblers, tits, flycatchers, thrushes, woodpeckers and tawny owls. Although large, acorns are consumed by woodpigeons, jays and grey squirrels. In old trees, the many capacious holes become homes for birds, including brown owls, barn owls and woodpeckers. It is a combination of an animal boarding house and a living larder when grown in Britain, but take it to Australia and it will be a barren paradise. In each country plants and animals have evolved together. Evergreen oaks from the Mediterranean, the Turkey oak (with mossy acorn cups), the holm oak (with oval leaves) and the willow oak (leaves long and narrow) are all decorative, but they contribute little to the British food chain.

HISTORICAL AND OTHER USES Oak is so prominent in the folklore and history of England that it is used as a synonym for solidness: 'Heart-of-oak are our ships, heart-of-oak are our men.' The fattening of hogs on acorns was such an important branch of domestic economy that at the end of the seventh century King Ina enacted laws for its regulation. Oak woods were preserved not just for fuel and timber, but to feed pigs, which devoured acorns and also beech-mast. As pigs have litters of up to ten, they were the sustenance of all classes. Even in Elizabethan times, swine ran wild over the fells of Lancashire and Cumberland and in the Weald of Kent. St Bright at Kildare built her church under an oak which still stood in the tenth century and gave its name to the town, from Irish *Cill-dara*, church of the oak. Oak was the main source of tannin from Neolithic times until the fifteenth century when it was superseded by sumac from the East.

Because of its elasticity, oak was so much used in shipbuilding that the trees were known as the 'wooden walls of England'. In 1588, Philip of Spain ordered his Armada soldiers, if they landed, to burn and destroy every oak in the Forest of Dean. When ships were old, their timber was often recycled into timber-framed houses, especially in East Anglia: Coggeshall, Ely and Stebbing are good examples. Lord Nelson planted acorns to sustain the fleet in future centuries; timber from some of those now mature oaks was used to repair his famous ship HMS *Victory* as part of his bicentenary celebrations in 2005. A vast wooden disc dating from the reign of Edward I, made from a single slice of oak cut from an enormous bole, has hung on the wall of the great Hall of Winchester Castle for six hundred years; it is designated, quite incorrectly, as King Arthur's Round Table. Oak is still used widely as timbers for churches and the repair of early houses, and in the furniture and coffin trade; among the famous people buried in oak coffins was the actor Sir Laurence Olivier, in

1989. J. and F. J. Baker and Co., in Colyton, Devon, is Britain's last remaining traditional oak bark tanner.

During the Civil War, Prince Charles hid from the Roundheads in a hollow oak in Boscobel, Shropshire; his Restoration as King Charles II in 1660 is celebrated on Oak-Apple Day, 29 May. An oak spray used to appear on one side of British sixpences and shillings, until it was changed for the British lion.

NAME Latin *quercus*, a generic term for an acorn-bearing trees, derived from Celtic *quer*, fine, and *cuez*, tree.

OTHER SPECIES Sessile oak (*Quercus petraea*) differs in having higher growth on a straighter trunk and a less spreading habit. It suits sandy or acid soils. Reaching a maximum height of 42m/138ft, this large and long-lived tree is really suitable only for a large garden. While *Q. robur* is more widespread in the south, *Q. petraea* grows in the west and north of Britain. The easiest way of distinguishing them is in spring when they come into bloom. The flowers and acorns of *Q. robur* are borne on stalks, while in *Q. petraea* they are stalkless.

Rhamnus cathartica (Rhamnaceae)

BUCKTHORN, COMMON BUCKTHORN, PURGING BUCKTHORN

Hicum, peridicum, all clothed in green
The King could not tell it, no more could the Queen
So they sent to consult wise men from the East
Who said it had horns, though it was not a beast
    Riddle, quoted by Alice M. Coats,
    'Garden Shrubs and their Histories'
    The answer is buck's horn (buckthorn)

Buckthorn is generally a problem-free shrub well suited to small gardens, particularly in towns, making it useful for a dry, chalky garden. Thorny and deciduous, it has dense branches of small greenish-yellow flowers followed by globular berries about the size of peas, black and shining when ripe. It grows in sun or semi-shade and is fairly tolerant of most soils, although it prefers free-draining, alkaline soil. The berries are purgative but not very poisonous. It can be grown as a free-standing tree or as part of a hedge. For berries, five or six female trees should be planted for every one male.

GROWTH HABIT A bushy deciduous shrub, usually up to 5m/16½ft high (though a few specimens can reach twice that), with thick foliage growing from near the ground.

PROPAGATION It is easily grown from fruits gathered in autumn, sown in nursery beds in February, lined out the following autumn and grown on for up to two years before planting out permanently. Semi-hardwood cuttings with a heel can be taken in late summer, or the plant can be layered in spring.

ROLE IN LANDSCAPE Buckthorn occurs in woods, scrub and hedgerows on calcareous soils in the south, east and midlands of England; it is common on the dry heights of southern chalk downs but is also found as far north as the Lake District and the Tees.

TRUNK AND BARK The rough bark is grey-brown, almost black on the young twigs, and the shoots are either longer growth shoots or short leaf and flower shoots.

LEAVES From April dull green, rounded egg-shaped leaves appear, up to 7cm/3in long, finely toothed at the edges, each with three to four pairs of lateral veins curving towards the tip. They turn brownish-yellow in autumn. They can attract crown rust, seen as orange specks – this also attacks cereals, so it is best not to plant buckthorn near arable land.

BUDS, FLOWERS AND FRUIT Inconspicuous clusters of tiny, four-petalled, yellowish-green flowers appear at the base of the leaf stalk in spring, male and female on separate plants. From September the female plant carries an abundant crop of pea-sized fruits, each with three or four seeds, green at first but ripening to shiny black and often remaining on the bush after leaf fall. Buds and leaves are arranged in opposite pairs, the leaves almost at right angles to the stem, often ending in a stout spine.

PLANT–ANIMAL RELATIONSHIPS Buckthorn, along with alder buckthorn, is the foodplant of the brimstone butterfly; the larvae of the green hairstreak sometimes also feed on it. The berries are eaten by wintering birds.

HISTORICAL AND OTHER USES The wood was once used for charcoal to be turned into gunpowder for old flintlock guns. It was stripped of bark, aged for two years and cooked in huge furnaces.

NAME From Greek *rhamnos*, branch. The common name, first used by Lyte in 1578, is a translation of *cervi spina*, buck's thorn, the name given to it by early botanists. The black berries were a purgative in herbal and veterinary medicine.

Ribes nigrum (Grossulariaceae)

BLACKCURRANT

Blackcurrant is mostly grown in gardens for its fruit, used in cooking or making jam. The Tree Council recommends its thorny shrubs and brambles as a deterrent to thieves, and to protect newly planted trees in public areas.

GROWTH HABIT It grows up to 2m/7ft in height.

PROPAGATION The seeds can remain dormant in the soil for long periods until the right conditions for germination are present.

ROLE IN LANDSCAPE Often known by the perfume of its buds and leaves and its long, thorny, pliable, arching stems, it is said to be a true native only in Yorkshire and the Lake District; elsewhere its presence is due to the agency of birds and man.

TRUNK, BARK AND BRANCHES Short lateral branches.

LEAVES Leaves are 3–10cm/1–4in in diameter, glabrous to sparsely pubescent, with more pointed lobes than in redcurrant, and not scented as in other species.

BUDS, FLOWERS AND FRUIT Clusters of five-petalled pinky-white to greenish-yellow flowers appear between May and September and develop into edible black globular berries.

PLANT–ANIMAL RELATIONSHIPS The berries are eaten by wintering birds. Thrushes often devour them, then wipe their bills on the leaves to brush off the seeds. A variety of moth caterpillars and beetles chew their way through the leaves including the currant pug, magpie, phoenix, spinach and v-moth. Like many other wild plants, its size is kept in check by rabbits eating the tender shoots and seedlings.

HISTORICAL AND OTHER USES Juice from the berries, rich in Vitamin C, is commercially important in cordials and drinks, especially in France for *crème de cassis*. The leaves have joined the berries as the base for a commercially manufactured cordial, and are also sold as a herbal tea. Once the stems were used to tie thatch and bundles of brushwood. An essential oil is extracted from the flower buds, and another, rich in fatty acids, from the seeds.

NAME As with many names there is controversy over its origins. The generic name *Ribes* could be from Danish *ribs* or Swedish *risp*, since the currant is primarily a northern European family, or from an ancient Arabic word connected with rhubarb.

OTHER SPECIES

GOOSEBERRY (*Ribes uva-crispa*), often found growing thick and wild in derelict parts of old gardens, is used by willow wrens, robins, blackbirds and thrushes for nesting. A hardy plant, gooseberry is tolerant of shade and grows well under taller fruit trees, but in shade it needs a little more space. It grows well in various soils, so long as they are not waterlogged; slight acidity is preferred, but it dislikes sites susceptible to late spring frosts. It is healthier if given a little potash and nitrogen (from manure, compost, urine, seaweed or from mulching with plenty of comfrey leaves). It is best pruned in winter to achieve an open, goblet or cup-shaped bush with six to eight main branches. Netting is used by some gardeners to protect buds from birds in winter and the fruit in summer. Gooseberry sawfly can be a serious problem, but less so if a garden is rich in biodiversity; interplanting with broad beans is said to help deter sawfly.

Gooseberries can be propagated in late September by cuttings taken from strong shoots of the summer's growth which should be about 30cm/1ft long with all the buds intact. The unripe shoot tip should be cut off just above a bud and the base trimmed just below a bud; stick in 16cm/6in deep, best through a mulch. Alternatively, it can be reproduced with 13cm/5in cuttings taken from half-ripe wood in July or August, preferably with a heel or layering.

Delicious raw when ripe, or cooked in pies and tarts, gooseberry is the earliest major fruit to ripen and is high in Vitamin A and potassium. Really old trees, however, put out only hard green berries, but these can be made into jelly flavoured with elderflowers. Ripe fruits do not keep well; unripe fruits store for a week or so. Gooseberries are long-lasting bushes, with a yield of 3.5–4.5kg/8–10lb of fruit annually for twenty to thirty years.

The common name is often said to be from its traditional use in sauce to accompany goose, but the late Geoffrey Grigson, *Dictionary of English Plant Names,* disagreed, claiming it comes from the French *groseille,* redcurrant, or its sixteenth-century botanical Latinisation, *grossula.* He quotes Turner, 1548: 'Uva crispa is also called Grossularia, in English a Groser bushe, a Goosebery bush.'

Also: Redcurrant (*Ribes rubrum*) and downy currant (*Ribes spicatum*).

Rosa arvensis (Rosaceae)

FIELD ROSE

And I will make thee beds of roses
With a thousand fragrant posies,
And a cop of flowers and a kirtle
Embroider'd all with leaves of myrtle.
    'The Passionate Shepherd to his Love', Christopher Marlowe (1564–93)

This decorative shrub enhances hedges, trellises or shrub borders. Smaller and less vigorous than the dog-rose, it is tolerant of cutting back and more suited to small gardens. It grows in sun or shade, but needs sun in order to flower and fruit, and in most garden soils, preferably deep or clay soils, not very acid or wet. Shakespeare, who mentioned roses in over seventy plays and sonnets, spoke about many suffering from 'killing frosts' and the ravages of the canker worm. Queen Titania in *A Midsummer Night's Dream* sends elves to 'kill cankers in the musk-rose buds'.

GROWTH HABIT With the support of neighbouring plants, field rose can reach up to 2m/7ft, but in an open spot it forms a low, spreading mound of arching stems.

PROPAGATION Field rose can be propagated from seeds extracted from hips which should be gathered when ripe and broken open to expose the contents. Seeds should be stored in moist sand outside, protected from mice, until sown in nursery rows. The following autumn the seedlings should be thinned; one to two years later they should be planted in a permanent site. It is also quite easy to strike cuttings, but seeds are better as they provide a more varied genetic background.

ROLE IN LANDSCAPE With the aid of its prickles, this deciduous, trailing or climbing rose scrambles through hedges and bushes in hedgerows, scrub, woodland clearings or lightly shaded woods, on all but the most acid or waterlogged soils. The colour contrast between the sides of the stem and the persistent red hips in autumn makes it distinctive in hedgerows. It is distinguished from *Rosa canina* by the union of the styles in the flowers into a long slender column.

TRUNK, BARK AND BRANCHES Its climbing branches have slender stems, usually hairless but armed with hooked prickles.

LEAVES The stems are purple on the sunlit side and green in the shade, and the leaves have five to seven oval, shining, green, toothed leaflets which are hairy on the veins beneath.

BUDS, FLOWERS AND FRUIT In June and July clusters of white scentless flowers appear, each up to 5cm/2in across with five notched petals and a yellow centre featuring a column of joined styles as long as the stamens. This persists as a little spike at the top of the small round or oval red hips which ripen in October and often remain after leaf fall.

PLANT–ANIMAL RELATIONSHIPS *Rosa arvensis* may be visited by two kinds of leaflet-rolling insects: gall midges which fold the leaf upwards so that the underside encloses their fly-like maggots, and little black sawflies which fold the leaflets downwards, with the top side enclosing their caterpillar-like larvae. Caterpillars of the small quaker moth may also feed on the leaflets. The hips provide autumn food for birds, wood mice and foxes.

HISTORICAL AND OTHER USES Rosewater, distilled from rose petals, was used for washing the face and hands; dew from rose petals was highly prized as an ingredient in cosmetics in Elizabethan England. During the Wars of the Roses (1455–85), the House of York used a white rose (*Rosa arvensis*) as its symbol, the House of Lancaster a red (*Rosa canina*). Arthur Fox-Davies, *A Complete Guide to Heraldry* (1939), writes of these symbols: 'They are said to have been first assumed by John of Gaunt, Duke of Lancaster, and his brother Edmund, Duke of York. Both these roses were sometimes surrounded with rays, and termed *en soleil*, and later on they were frequently conjoined.' The emblem of the Tudors, which remains the symbol of British royalty to this day, is a single, five-petalled, pink rose, the colour embodying the uniting of the two factions.

NAME Latin *Rosa* from Greek and Celtic words meaning red.

Rosa canina (Rosaceae)
DOG-ROSE

Unkempt about those hedges blows,
An English unofficial rose
   'The Old Vicarage, Grantchester',
   Rupert Brooke (1887–1915)

Dog-rose is delightful either as a garden shrub or a rambling climber trained on a trellis, over an arbour or a decaying tree, or as a dense hedge or over an existing hedge where a darker green background will set off its pale pink flowers, red hips and arching stems. It flourishes in full sun, and may grow in shade but without flowering. Tolerant of most soil types, dog-rose accepts most garden soils as long as they are not water-logged or too dry, but prefers a rich moisture-retentive medium in a sunny or partially shaded situation. It is hardy and tolerates cutting back.

GROWTH HABIT The curved spines enable it to catch on to surrounding shrubs for support and it can reach more than 3m/10ft in height, but more often grows only up to 2m/7ft.

PROPAGATION Propagate as for field roses.

ROLE IN LANDSCAPE Dog-rose is found in hedgerows, scrub and wood-lands on a wide range of soils up to 550m/1,800ft. The gracefully arching stems of this beautiful deciduous suckering shrub, the largest of the English roses, has stout hooked prickles and a thickened base, and carries scented, shell-pink flowers. These combine to give the dog-rose qualities of vigour and delicacy which have inspired English poets for centuries.

TRUNK, BARK AND BRANCHES Climbing branches with hooked prickles of various shapes and sizes.

LEAVES Each stalked leaf has two to three opposite pairs of usually hairless, oval or elliptical, toothed leaflets with a larger terminal leaflet.

BUDS, FLOWERS AND FRUIT The fragrant, pale pink or white five-petalled flowers appear singly or in small clusters on spiny stems in June or July, each up to 5cm/2in across, with numerous stamens around a central cluster of separate, hairy styles. Narrow green sepals usually have a frill of side lobes. They turn into glossy, scarlet, egg-shaped hips, which fully ripen in October or November.

PLANT–ANIMAL RELATIONSHIPS The flowers are pollinated by bees, beetles and thrips, and the hips are a food source for many animals, from foxes and wood mice to birds, especially blackbirds. Gall-wasps produce balls of crimson 'moss' on the leaf stalks (called 'Robin's pin-cushions') and smooth or spiked pea galls on the leaflets. As well as spangle and silk-button galls on the leaves, there are frequently the much larger marble galls, which resemble brown marbles and cling to the twigs.

HISTORICAL AND OTHER USES The hips are rich in Vitamin C and are used in jelly and syrup. During World War II, children were nationally encouraged to pick them to make syrup, to assist their health during food rationing.

NAME Latin *Rosa* from Greek and Celtic words meaning red; Latin *canina*, dog.

Rosa pimpinellifolia (Rosaceae)

BURNET ROSE

Gather ye rose-buds while ye may,
Old Time is still a-flying:
And this same flower that smiles to-day,
To-morrow will be dying.
    'Gather ye rose-buds', Robert Herrick (1591–1674)

A charming, bushy little deciduous shrub, burnet rose could be called the seaside rose as it flourishes on sand and limestone near coasts. Low-growing and vigorous with spreading suckers and creamy-white, occasionally pink, flowers, its stems are covered with fine prickles rather than the sharp spines borne by other roses. In contrast to scarlet hips, the fruit turns purplish-black when ripe. Burnet rose flourishes in an open, sunny site, but does not like wet areas. It tolerates very dry conditions and looks good in shrub borders, on dry banks or in large rock gardens. It prefers free-draining soil, preferably alkaline, growing best in natural calcareous soils that contains some lime. Although it is ideal as a low-growing shrub or in a tub, it suckers freely and needs controlling, but this tendency can be used to advantage if it is planted as ground cover.

GROWTH HABIT Low-growing, seldom above 60cm/24in in height, it has upright, much-branched woody stems armed with masses of straight, slender prickles intermixed with stiff bristles.

PROPAGATION Burnet rose is easily propagated by separating the suckers in autumn.

ROLE IN LANDSCAPE Found mainly in dunes and sandy places around the coasts, including the Outer Hebrides, and locally on inland heaths and downland, ascending to 450m/1,475ft in the Pennines, it also occurs in limestone areas and on sandy heaths.

TRUNK, BARK AND BRANCHES Short branches up to 2m/7ft, with slender, prickly, purple-brown spines.

LEAVES The leaves have three to five pairs of toothed oval leaflets with finely toothed edges and a terminal leaflet, each 5–20mm/¼–¾in long.

BUDS, FLOWERS AND FRUIT From May to July the bushes are smothered in creamy-white, rarely pink, flowers up to 4cm/1½in across which appear singly at the tips of the stems. Each has five broad, notched petals and numerous golden stamens at the centre. The leathery, round hips are crowned with long sepals and ripen to blackish-purple in September.

PLANT–ANIMAL RELATIONSHIPS The flowers are pollinated by bees, beetles and thrips. The leaf stalks and mid-rib are attacked by gall-wasps which produce pea galls, and the leaflets may be mined by the larvae of small moths. The hips are eaten by many birds, including blackbirds.

HISTORICAL AND OTHER USES Like other wild roses it is famed as an excellent source of Vitamin C, in the form of rosehip syrup.

NAME From Latin *Pimpinella saxifraga*, a member of the carrot family, which its leaves are thought to resemble. The common name plays on its resemblance to burnet-saxifrage; in 1731 Miller described it as a 'wild burnet-leaved Rose'.

OTHER SPECIES which are cultivated occasionally include small-leaved sweet-briar (*R. agrestis*), glaucous or hairy dog-rose (*R. caesia*), soft downy rose (*R. mollis*), round-leaved dog-rose (*R. obtusifolia*), Sherard's downy rose (*R. sherardi*), short-styled field-rose (*R. stylosa*) and sweet-briar (*R. rubiginosa*), also known as eglantine.

Eglantine is a wild rose with bright pink flowers which derives its name from the Old French for 'prickly' and 'thorny'; it is a rather uncommon native species of basic soils. Occasionally, it grows from the ground with a single stem but more usually as an erect, multi-stemmed bush with heavy, sharp spines. It suits most gardens and can be grown as a small bush, added to a hedge or trained up a wall or trellis. Like the dog-rose it is long-flowering and similar in growth but has hooked prickles, and prefers a more open sunny situation and drier types of soil. While dog-roses can tolerate a wider range of soils, sweet-briar prefers some lime. Neither species has scented flowers, but the sweet-briar has tiny brown glands on the under-surface of the leaves that make it fragrant when rubbed. Since the sixteenth century, the word briar in literature has been generally used to distinguished wild from cultivated roses.

From this bleeding hand of mine
Take this sprig of eglantine
Which, though sweet unto your smell,
Yet the fretful briar will tell,
He who plucks the sweets shall prove
Many thorns to be in love.
    'The Sprig of Eglantine Given to a Maid', Robert Herrick (1591–1674)

Rubus fruticosus (Rosaceae)

BLACKBERRY, BRAMBLE

How oft, my slice of pocket store consumed,
Still hungering, penniless and far from home,
I fed on scarlet hips and stony haws,
Or blushing crabs, or berries, that emboss
The bramble, black as jet, or sloes austere.
  'The Charm of the Country' from 'The Task',
  William Cowper (1731–1800)

Gardeners may balk at cultivating bramble because it can quickly form a dense, unwieldy mass. It definitely has no role in the formal parts of gardens, but with its white or pink flowers it can be eye-catching in wilder areas, if controlled with pruning and training. There are now many cultivars which produce heavy-cropping varieties of blackberries, but the fruit is often not as delicious as its wild ancestor. It needs some support: if there is no available wall, fence or trellis, it can be grown up a stout post, around which the main shoots can be loosely tied. Neither the plant nor its hook-like prickles should be allowed to interfere with other plants. If the arching stems reach the ground they root at their tips, so that the plant becomes even more invasive than it is normally. To check its spread, cut out old stems after the second season and remove suckers and seedlings.

Bramble tolerates a wide range of well-drained soils, from acid to alkaline, with loamy soil suiting it best. It is best grown against a sunny wall so that the fruit ripens; it tolerates semi-shade but will not grow in deep shade. Cultivation presents few problems as long as it is encouraged to grow as a climber and not along the ground, and it is not allowed to be invasive. On good soil the shoots can scramble over 4m/13ft up a tree. In small gardens it is best if grown in a reasonably large container, making it easier to control. It can also make a good addition to a hedge, forming an effective barrier and deterrent against burglars. A vigorous woody climber, with angled stems armed with spines, it is instantly recognisable, but exact species are difficult to identify: there are over 400 microspecies, all with similar growth.

GROWTH HABIT It can grow to 2m/7ft or more.

PROPAGATION Propagation is often by rooted stem tips, deliberately induced by pegging down shoots, layering the tips and cutting off the rooted pieces in spring and growing on.

ROLE IN LANDSCAPE Bramble is common in woodland in hedgerows and scrub throughout Britain. There are few areas, even well up in the Scottish mountains, where it cannot be found.

TRUNK, BARK AND BRANCHES Its tough, arching stems (stolons) are armed with prickles. Young stems often have beautiful colouring, from deep purple through red to pale green.

LEAVES The small deciduous leaves – oval, toothed and rough to the touch – are in groups of three to five, open in April and turn crimson, scarlet, orange, yellow or bronze in autumn. In sheltered spots they may stay on the plant through the winter.

BUDS, FLOWERS AND FRUIT Panicles of pretty, five-petalled white flowers, often suffused with pink, surround the anthers carrying yellow pollen, and appear from May to September. Once the flowers fade, the small, hard brown fruit slowly swells and changes: the familiar fruit is a group of many one-seeded drupes, green at first then ripening from red to glossy black in autumn. There was a superstition that one should not eat wild blackberries after 1 October, because by then the Devil has spat on them – i.e. they have begun to shrivel and taste bad.

PLANT–ANIMAL RELATIONSHIPS Bramble blossoms are a rich source of pollen throughout summer, their spreading petals forming landing stages for bees. They also provide nectar for butterflies, including the peacock, small tortoiseshell and comma, and other insects. Among the wide range of insects attracted to bramble are shield-bugs and green hairstreak butterflies which lay eggs on the leaves. The plant makes excellent cover for nesting birds which, together with small mammals, eat the fruits.

HISTORICAL AND OTHER USES At the end of summer the fruit is abundant and delicious – it has many culinary uses and can be mixed with wind-fallen apples to make jelly. Once the stems were cut in half, cleaned and made into twine for making brooms and baskets.

NAME The common name is derived from Old English *braembel*; the root *brom* means a thorny shrub (as in *broom*).

OTHER SPECIES

CLOUDBERRY *Rubus chamaemorus*

This has creeping underground stems and often forms large patches over the ground. Although it is related to bramble and raspberry, cloudberry is easily distinguished as it does not have any spines or prickles and is much smaller. This plant of mountain and moor occurs in most high mountainous areas except the south-west of Scotland and the Outer Hebrides. It is ideal for rockeries where it will form thin ground cover and can survive in very dry sites, but it may be difficult to obtain either in seed or plant form. Male and female flowers are both white and look similar but are borne on separate parts. The fruit is red at first, then becomes orange as it ripens. The berries are relished by birds of the high mountains. It is the plant badge of MacFarlane clan.

RASPBERRY *Rubus idaeus*

A deciduous shrub which grows to around 2m/7ft in semi-shade or no shade; it needs moist soil. Its pretty white hermaphrodite flowers are pollinated by bees and flies and are in bloom from July to September. The tasty ripe fruits are picked for jams and desserts. Mostly modern cultivars are now grown in gardens, and native raspberry bushes are found usually in the wild, in woods and heaths throughout the British Isles. Plants like well-drained, acidic soil (not chalky) and if left to themselves form thickets of long, climbing vines. The stems, just under 2m/7ft, are only slightly prickly.

DEWBERRY *Rubus caesius*

This small shrub, with moderate prickles and berries similar in appearance to raspberries but blue instead of red, is occasionally cultivated in gardens and is distinguished by its large white flowers. It has thin, glaucous stems and slender three-lobed leaves.

Ruscus aculeatus (Liliaceae)

BUTCHER'S BROOM

I saw a crag, a lofty stone
As ever tempest beat!
Out of its head an Oak had grown,
A Broom out of its feet.
The time was March, a cheerful noon –
The thaw-wind, with the breath of June,
Breathed gently from the warm south-west.
    'The Oak and the Broom', William Wordsworth (1770–1850)

This small, neat evergreen shrub is a stunning sight when covered with round, red berries – 10–12mm/½in in diameter, looking like little balls stuck in the middle of the 'false leaf' or modified shoot (cladode). A member of the lily family, it is not related to the yellow-flowered broom but, like its namesake, is hardy, thriving in almost any soil or situation. As it remains green after deciduous trees have shed their leaves, it is often planted in shrubberies or on the edges of woods on well-drained soils and in rocky or stony ground, especially its preferred chalk. A really determined plant, it needs to be kept in check.

GROWTH HABIT In the range of 25cm–1m/10–39in.

PROPAGATION Propagation is generally effected by division of the roots in autumn. Seeds are a superior method, but slower: germination can be erratic and it usually takes two to three years before seedlings are large enough to plant permanently. When planted under trees, it soon spreads into large clumps.

ROLE IN LANDSCAPE Native to woods, hedgerows, rocky and dry places from sea level up to 1,000m/3,300ft. The poem above by Wordsworth was inspired when he was walking on a mountain pathway from Upper Rydal to Grasmere, where broom grows under a crag on a block of stone. As it is spiny and tough, it withstands sheep and other animals.

TRUNK, BARK AND BRANCHES Much-branched, erect, dark green stems rise from rhizomes that creep along the ground.

LEAVES The leaves are minute and the parts that we might take to be leaves are, in fact, modified leaves known as cladodes. The petiole, the true leaf, is ovate to lanceolate in shape and ends with a sharp little spine.

BUDS, FLOWERS AND FRUIT The flowers, greenish and somewhat inconspicuous, open from January to April. Female flowers have six lobes, with the inner three smaller than the outer. Male flowers have three joined stamens. The fruit ripens in autumn and often remains on the shrub through the winter months.

PLANT–ANIMAL RELATIONSHIPS Female plants produce bright red berries which are eaten by birds. The spotted ladybird hibernates on the shoots.

HISTORICAL AND OTHER USES Butchers used bunches of dried twigs for scouring boards, blocks and benches, and also to make fly-whisks. The young roots were once cooked and eaten like another member of the lily family, asparagus.

NAME The Latin name was used by Virgil; the common name is derived from its use. In the nineteenth century, sirloin steaks were decorated by butchers at Christmas with the red-berried stems. See also broom (*Cytisus scoparius*).

Salix alba (Salicaceae)

WHITE WILLOW

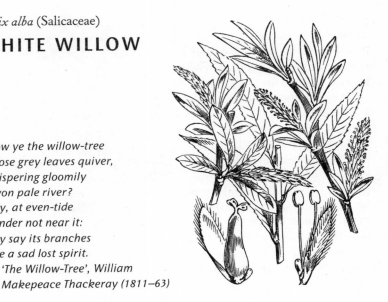

Know ye the willow-tree
Whose grey leaves quiver,
Whispering gloomily
To yon pale river?
Lady, at even-tide
Wander not near it:
They say its branches
Hide a sad lost spirit.
   'The Willow-Tree', William
   Makepeace Thackeray (1811–63)

Many gardeners plant willow for quick results: in the right conditions, some grow as much as 3m/10ft in a year. White willow catkins appear at the same time as the leaves: the twigs, covered with a distinctive white sheen, are a magnificent sight. It is an excellent tree for any large garden, particularly in its natural habitat beside water; its silvery leaves are particularly graceful when the breeze ruffles them. William Robinson wrote in *The Wild Garden*: 'our native Willows . . . are not merely as good as any of the garden [cultivated] Willows but as good in beauty as the Olive tree – even where the Olive is most beautiful'. With their 'slender wands and silvery leaves against the summer sky they are the prettiest things in the winter landscape'. White willow prefers an open site and deep, well-drained, moist loam or peat soil; it will not thrive on thin, chalky soils. Owing to its water-seeking roots, it should not be planted near drains or close to a house. It is a tradition to pollard white willow, so it often appears smaller than it is in the wild. It tolerates cutting back and also pollution.

GROWTH HABIT Can eventually reach a height of around 25m/80ft.

PROPAGATION Willows are often better propagated from seed and worth the effort. Care and speed are needed, as the seeds of willows lose their vitality within a week at ordinary temperatures (they will last longer at a low temperature). Seeds must be extracted from the down and sown immediately on the surface of sterile compost, kept moist at all times. Most willows are also easily propagated from hardwood cuttings, taken in winter and grown on for a year or so, or from two-year-old stems inserted *in situ*. The ease with which willow cuttings strike is due to the presence of rudimentary roots already developed within the tissues of the parent plant in the stem. Once leaves have appeared on the new plants they can be hardened off before being transferred into potting compost, lining out in autumn and growing on for up to two years.

ROLE IN LANDSCAPE White willow grows along the wet banks of streams and ponds in lowland areas, especially in wooded river valleys, marshes and beside lowland rivers, streams and ponds throughout England, but is more common in the East Midlands and East Anglia. Often pollarded, it is usually thought of as a small tree. Different species and sub-species hybridise freely, making it difficult to identify.

TRUNK, BARK AND BRANCHES The grey bark on the stout trunk is closely ridged and fissured. The main branches are erect, carrying smaller, spreading branches with young, downy twigs which become shiny brown, pink or yellow.

LEAVES The alternate leaves, up to 10cm/4in long, whitish, short-stalked, are narrowly lance-shaped with pointed tips and toothed margins, pale green above, a pale bluish-green beneath and covered when young with silky, silvery hairs which are denser on the underside. In autumn the leaves change colour and drop in sequence, so the tree never becomes completely yellow.

BUDS, FLOWERS AND FRUIT In April and May, after the leaves, the yellow male catkins, up to 5cm/2in long, together with the stalkless green female catkins, appear on separate trees. The female quickly produces fluffy fruits which are distributed by summer winds.

PLANT–ANIMAL RELATIONSHIPS Like other willows, the leaves are hosts to many insects including a sawfly that induces the formation of 'bean galls' on the leaf blade which tend to be red above and green below.

HISTORICAL AND OTHER USES The wood is pliant and easily worked. White willow stems were used for fencing and basket making while the light timber was used to make bowls, plates and baskets. A famous use of willow is the transformation of its salicylic acid into an anti-inflammatory and analgesic, the forerunner of aspirin and other painkillers. At the National Willow Collection, at the IACR Rothamsted Experimental Station near Harpenden, Hertforshire (started at Long Ashton Research Station in 1922), members of the public can view the trees from a public footpath that runs alongside the site. One modern use of willows is in environmentally friendly coffins, available from the Sawd Partnership in Sittingbourne, Kent (www.bamboocoffins.co.uk).

NAME Latin *Salix*, willow.

OTHER SPECIES Cricket bat willow (*Salix alba*, var. *cærulea*) is a cultivated timber from which cricket bats are made. It grows in wetland plantations in Essex, Suffolk and Norfolk. The leaves are uniformly blue-grey on both sides.

Salix caprea (Salicaceae)

GOAT WILLOW, PUSSY WILLOW, GREAT SALLOW

Now while I cannot hear the city's din;
Now while the early budders are just nev
And run in mazes of the youngest hue
About old forests; while the willow trails
Its delicate amber; and the dairy pails
Bring home increase of milk . . .
'Endymion', John Keats (1795–1821)

Goat willow is famous for its fluffy yellow catkins during the latter end of March and grey silky buds in late autumn. Despite being a multi-stemmed bush that grows in the wild near or on river banks, this fast-growing, tall, graceful tree can adapt in gardens to become a standard, where its grey-green appearance makes it an interesting contrast to deeper shades of green. It tolerates drier conditions than other native willows, and withstands pollution and cutting back. A good-natured plant, easy to grow as a tree or a shrub, freestanding or in a mixed hedge, it quickly makes a handsome show in moist situations. One drawback, however, is its spreading habit – it needs to be in a large garden or must receive regular coppicing. It prefers a light, sunny spot and grows on most well-drained soils. This is the species Walter de la Mare could have been describing when he wrote: 'Leans now the fair willow, dreaming amid her locks of green . . .' It was traditionally used in certain areas of England as a living fence: stems are planted in the ground and woven gently as the tree grows to the desired height – a fine leafy hedge can be achieved in a short time.

GROWTH HABIT Not usually more than 5m/16½ft but it is capable of growing to 10m/33ft (some specimens even double this height). It has a tendency to spread, sometimes leaning until branches touch the ground and take root.

PROPAGATION Desmond Meikle, *Willows and Poplars of Great Britain*, explains that the traditional way of growing willows, by pushing green sticks into the ground, does not work with goat willows, which should be grown from fresh seed. When the fruits open they disperse hundreds of seeds, each attached to long, silver-white hairs that help their passage in the wind as they are blown around the countryside.

ROLE IN LANDSCAPE Goat willow is found in mixed, broad-leaved woodland, hedgerows and scrub, most often on basic soils, throughout England, ascending to 500m/1,650ft in the Pennines. It is the most intensively managed, commercial wetland species in Britain – and, unlike agricultural crops, is grown and harvested in a traditional way. Hardy and versatile, it is often seen by streams and the banks of canals as it is sometimes grown to stop water erosion.

TRUNK, BARK AND BRANCHES The short trunk has smooth, greenish-brown bark, fissured when old. While the young downy twigs are grey-haired, winter twigs are hairless and shiny. The many wide branches form a rounded outline.

LEAVES The soft leaves, up to 10cm/4in long, are oval to rounded with a wavy margin and a short point, alternate, greyish-green above and pale grey with silky hairs on the underside.

BUDS, FLOWERS AND FRUIT Like nearly all willows, goat willow is dioecious, i.e. it has male and female flowers on the same trees. First to open are the slender, light-green female flower heads which later carry the seed capsules covered in silvery down. Next are the silky, grey, bud-like male catkins – usually smothered with showy golden anthers. They appear in March and April before the leaves.

PLANT–ANIMAL RELATIONSHIPS The catkins are a source of early pollen and nectar. The leaves, branches and bark harbour over 200 insect species, making the goat willow Britain's second most hospitable tree, after oak. These include beetles, bees, hoverflies and ants, making it a favourite with insectivorous birds. The yellow glands at the base of the male catkins produce nectar that attracts large tortoiseshell and comma butterflies, as well as peacocks and brimstones, and the anthers supply pollen for bees. Caterpillars feed on the foliage, including the dramatic

purple emperor butterfly whose larvae pupate beneath the leaves, and the caterpillars of the poplar, sallow kitten, buff-tip, common Quaker and puss moths, which in turn become food for birds such as tits. In late March to April, the trees are often busy with quite large flocks of siskins and play host to many visiting birds, including the chiffchaff and the willow warbler on its return from migration.

HISTORICAL AND OTHER USES Goat willow is still used as a living fence. Its pliant dried stems are used for wickerwork, and made into everything from hurdles, beehives and chair-backs to eel-traps and laundry baskets. It was also used for some tool handles and clothes pegs. It is not good firewood, having a tendency to 'spit' as it burns.

NAME Because so many features of this shrubby tree are softly downy or rounded like a cat, it earned the nickname 'pussy willow'. The name 'goat' comes from the young spring foliage being fed to goats.

OTHER SPECIES Almond willow (*Salix triandra*), which has long been cultivated for basket making, has fragrant male catkins and is similar to the goat willow but smaller, growing only to a maximum of 9m/30ft. Despite its preference for a wet environment, it is also eminently suitable for gardens.

Salix cinerea (Salicaceae)

GREY WILLOW, GREY SALLOW

When once the lover's rose is dead,
Or laid aside forlorn,
Then willow-garlands, 'bout the head,
Bewildered with tears, are worn.
    'To the Willow-Tree', Robert Herrick (1591–1674)

The intense grey on the underside of the long, broad leaves gives this willow a distinctive appearance. Experts can also distinguish it from the goat willow by little crest-like longitudinal prominences on the trunk. This large native shrub or small tree has contrasting red veins and abundant yellow catkins that appear in spring when the branches are still bare. Like most willows it thrives in damp or wet areas, such as the edge of ponds and slow-flowing rivers, but it is not fussy about soil. Grey willow can be grown as a small tree or clipped so that it remains a large shrub. Although it will tolerate an exposed or windy environment, it prefers partial shade or partial sun, rather than full sun. In the wild, it thrives on chalky soils and survives harsh coastal environments and winds, and is tolerant of acid and alkaline soils. It suits many gardens as it is able to withstand enthusiastic pruning.

ROLE IN LANDSCAPE Grey willow grows in almost any soil but really thrives in wet areas, especially near rivers; it is widespread in alluvial plains and fresh water wetlands. It is also found on lake margins, cut-out bogs, riversides and hedgerows, damp woods, fens and marshy places where moisture is readily available, such as drainage lines. As it tolerates much colder water than other willows, in some swampy areas its growth is so prolific that it is occasionally looked upon as a weed. It is the most common of all the *Salix* species in Northern Ireland.

GROWTH HABIT Usually 1–2m/39in–7ft, maximum 7m/22ft.

PROPAGATION Hardwood cuttings in late autumn usually root easily.

TRUNK, BARK AND BRANCHES The trunk is stout with grey-green branches and smooth bark. The shoots are grey or greenish-grey and remain hairy, or are reddish to dark purple, often becoming smooth.

LEAVES The *Salix* genus is characterised by the consistency of its leaves, a little like those of sage but of a different colour. In this species the leaves are broad and widest beyond the middle and the edges may be wavy; the upper surface is green and glabrous, the lower side silvery-white and downy. Each is about 2–7cm/¾–3in long by 1.5–3.5cm/½–1½in wide, shining on the upper surface and, due to a cover of soft grey hairs, grey underneath.

BUDS, FLOWERS AND FRUIT Separate male and female catkins, each cylindrical, 1.5–3.5cm/½–1½in long, appear in spring before the leaves, each a capsule with two valves, containing many tiny seeds. It flowers in September and October.

PLANT–ANIMAL RELATIONSHIPS Because of its early pollen, grey willow is of great value to bees and other insects. Like all of Britain's willows, it is hospitable to many insects– over 200 identified species are associated with it.

HISTORICAL AND OTHER USES Due to its tendency to crush rather than splinter, its wood has been used for artificial limbs, floors and wagon platforms. Its shoots, like those of other willows, have long been used as fodder. Willows were a favourite of William Morris and they appear in many of his designs, including the famous willow pattern wallpaper.

NAME Latin *Salix*, willow; *cinerea*, ash-coloured.

Salix fragilis

Surrey

RXXXXXX Xy XX del. Xp. XX. 1952

OTHER SPECIES

CRACK WILLOW *Salix fragilis*

Another streamside tree, which reaches 25m/80ft and also suits large gardens. Its name is derived from its first written description in 1670 by John Ray, who referred to the branches snapping or cracking off. The young branches are easily broken in the wind and will often root where they fall, especially in damp muddy soil. This is worth bearing in mind if you are using willow wood for stakes or fencing – unless they have been completely dried out they will quickly root and start to grow, even if you plant them upside down.

DWARF WILLOW *Salix herbacea*

A little Highland plant that forms a dense carpet, it is often said to be the 'smallest tree in the world', but this is deceptive: under the ground the rootstock stretches out over a largish area. It makes an excellent plant for a rock garden.

Also: downy willow (*S. lapponum*), dark-leaved willow (*S. mysinifolia*), bay willow (*S. pentandra*), tea-leafed willow (*S. phylicifolia*), purple willow (*S. purpurea*), creeping willow (*S. repens*), osier (*S. viminalis*).

Sambucus nigra (Caprifoliaceae)

ELDER

The shutter of time darkening ceaselessly
Has whisked away the foam of may and elder
And I realise how now, as every year before,
Once again the gay months have eluded me
  'August', Louis MacNeice (1907–63)

Gilbert White wrote: 'When the elder blows, summer is established.' Its broad flat-topped clusters of numerous creamy-white flowers are a sign that warm weather has arrived. Yet, lovely and useful though this shrub or small tree is, in spring the leaves and blossoms have a distinctive, slightly unpleasant smell. It grows everywhere, quickly establishing a habitat – even in the London Underground where light penetrates.

ROLE IN LANDSCAPE Elder is widespread in woods, hedgerows, scrub and rough ground throughout England, commonly on calcareous or nitrogen-rich soils. It is one of the most vigorous British trees, establishing itself with speed and soon laden with blossom followed by masses of glossy black berries on red stalks. It often grows around farmyards, especially where there is an accumulation of animal droppings, and in woodlands as an understorey to ash. Even though it is one of the few trees that rabbits find distasteful, it is often found around rabbit warrens where the soil is broken or disturbed, and enriched by droppings.

No other native tree grows with such rapidity in its early years than elder, so it is often planted in new gardens – in sun or semi-shade and on most moist but well-drained soils. Many people do not appreciate this plant outside its flowering season, but as long as there is sufficient space elder is adaptable, and can be grown quickly into a shrub, a free-standing tree or a hedge. John Parkinson, *Theatrum Botanicum* (1640), wrote that it was 'planted in all places, to serve for hedges, and partitions of grounds, vineyards etc.' William Robinson also recommended it, saying that a large elder, in flower or fruit, with its branches nearly touching the turf, 'was no mean object'. When damaged by hard frosts, it regenerates and is tolerant of pruning which it may need to keep it under control.

GROWTH HABIT Often more of a shrub than a tree, it is usually around 2m/6ft, but in a favourable spot it can grow to around 5m/16½ft.

PROPAGATION It can be raised from seeds extracted from the berries, stored in moist sand, sown outside in winter, and grown on before setting out in a permanent site a year later. Hardwood cuttings with a heel can be taken in autumn.

TRUNK AND BARK When mature, elder trunks are covered with thick, ridged, grey-brown bark. Young shoots arise almost from ground level, smooth at first with marked pores.

LEAVES The pinnate leaves, sometimes opening as early as January in a mild winter, have five to seven ovate to elliptical leaflets, each slightly toothed and opposite up to 9cm/3½in long. These occasionally last until December or, in sheltered spots, brave a late winter.

BUDS, FLOWERS AND FRUIT Both the clusters of yellow-white flowers and juicy dark purple berries are edible. In June and July the tiny, musk-scented, five-petalled flowers appear at the tips of young shoots in large flat panicles up to 20cm/8in across, followed in August and September by heavy, hanging bunches of round fruits, each containing up to five seeds. Birds eat the berries and spread them to odd corners where they can pop up as new trees.

PLANT–ANIMAL RELATIONSHIPS The flowers produce nectar which attracts pollinating flies and beetles as well as swallowtail moths. Blue tits eat the seeds and comma butterflies enjoy the juice of the fermenting berries. The early crop of autumn berries provides a feast for most resident birds including blackbirds, song thrushes, starlings and greenfinches. For summer visitors such as blackcaps they are a source of nourishment before they begin their long migratory journey home. Other visitors include garden warblers.

HISTORICAL AND OTHER USES Because the mature timber is very tough, elder had many uses, including skewers, pegs, spoons and toys. The tree produced dyes: black from the bark, green from the leaves and blue from the flowers. Hollow stems were transformed into primitive musical pipes or flutes (as with bamboo). Elder's most profitable by-product was, and still is, the flowers, which are edible – they can be dipped in batter and fried, or boiled to make jam, cordial or sparkling wine. Both flowers and fruit are rich in Vitamin C. A survey by the Royal Botanic Gardens, Kew, showed that retail sales of elder products (largely from wild plants) in 1996 amounted to some £10 million. Elderflower cordial is made commercially and sold widely in supermarkets. Flowers are stripped from the umbel stalks, added to water, then boiled with sugar and strained. These flowers were once described as 'the medicine chest of the country people'. In *The Merry Wives of Windsor*, Shakespeare rated elder highly: 'What says my Aesculapius? My Galen? My heart of Elder?' (Aesculapius was the god of medicine). Superstition surrounds this tree, especially in Ireland – many Irish will not cut it back, because the leaking sap is said to be the blood of witches.

NAME *Sambucus* from Greek *sambuke*, a musical instrument said to have been made from hollow elder stems. The common name is from Old English *aeld*, fire, since the hollow stems were also used as bellows. Old English *ellern*, *ellen* or *elle* is sometimes also found in place names.

OTHER SPECIES Dwarf elder (*Sambucus edulus*).

Solanum dulcamara (Solanaceae)

WOODY NIGHTSHADE, BITTERSWEET

Faire berries . . . very red when they be ripe, of a swete taste at the first, but after very unpleasant, of a strong savour; growing together in clusters like burnished corall
    John Gerard (1545–1607)

This climbing shrubby vine is found scrambling through hedges and over seaside shingle, in hedgerows and on moist grassy banks beside rivers, streams and ponds, displaying its vivid, star-shaped, purple and yellow flowers from June to September. The clusters of dramatic five-petalled flowers dangle from the stems, each eventually forming a red berry. Although generally regarded as a weed, it has value as a trailing garden climber if helped with a support. It will give a long show of colour when trained on a trellis or a sunny wall, or it can be threaded through a hedge where both flowers and fruit will add interest. It can also be grown over stone walls, twined through hazel twigs in a border or used as ground cover. As it has no hooks or twining stems, it relies on neighbouring plants, stones or simply the ground for support. When it dies back in winter, only the base remains woody. Tough and tolerant of dry conditions, it can put up with shade and grow in town gardens which do not get strong sunlight. It likes full sun and moist but well-drained soil, and dislikes damp areas or too much wind and exposure.

WARNING All parts of woody nightshade are poisonous – as are the green parts of its relative, the potato. Other members of the *Solanaceae* family include henbane, tomato, aubergine, capsicum, tobacco and mandrake – these all contain toxic alkaloids in potentially fatal quantities.

GROWTH HABIT Grows quickly into a low, climbing, scrambling, sprawling vine often draping low over trees and shrubs, reaching about 3m/10ft in length.

PROPAGATION The stems layer and sucker naturally and these ready-rooted parts can be used to produce new plants by dividing them. Stems will often form roots where they touch the ground and the rooted shoots can simply be removed and grown on. Soft or semi-hard cuttings are taken in summer.

ROLE IN LANDSCAPE This little-cultivated native member of the potato family is widely distributed in low-lying situations. It is found in hedges, damp woodlands, rough ground, fens, ditches, sides of ponds and on shingle beaches throughout lowland England, but is rarer in the northern counties, growing up to 310m/1,120ft in Durham.

TRUNK, BARK AND BRANCHES Light brown and thin with obvious lenticels.

LEAVES The ovate- to lance-shaped, alternate leaves, up to 9cm/3½in long, are pointed and sometimes have two small lobes or leaflets at the base.

BUDS, FLOWERS AND FRUIT From June to September, the branched clusters of flowers appear on stalks opposite the leaves, each up to 1.5cm/½in across with five, curved back, spear-shaped purple (occasionally white) petals and five yellow anthers joined to form a pointed cone in the centre. The glossy, bright red, egg-shaped or oval berries, up to 1.2cm/½in long, contain many rounded seeds.

PLANT—ANIMAL RELATIONSHIPS Woody nightshade has a specialised flower to attract bees, which vibrate their wings as they hang from the anther cone, causing pollen to be released from holes at the tips of the anthers.

HISTORICAL AND OTHER USES Woody nightshade is a source of the alkaloid solanine and the amorphous glucoside dulcamarine — both powerful narcotics that can cause paralysis if overdosed.

NAME Latin *Solanum* from *solor*, to ease, indicating its medicinal power; *dulcamara* from *dulcis*, sweet, and *amarus*, bitter, referring to the taste of the berries which changes from bitter to sweet when chewed (do not test!). It was called woody nightshade to distinguish it from deadly nightshade.

Sorbus aria (Rosaceae)

COMMON WHITEBEAM

Whitebeam is closely related to the rowan, but its flower clusters are larger. As its umbelliferous flowers and leaves flash silvery-white undersides when rustled by the wind, it is eye-catching, especially if planted in front of a dark evergreen tree. With its neat shape, this deciduous small tree or large shrub suits most gardens except the very small. It thrives on most well-drained soils from dry and chalky to acid, with a preference for those that are lime-rich and dry. It can be grown as a specimen tree or to enhance a woodland corner. As it tolerates exposure to salt-laden winds, it suits coastal gardens; in towns it copes well with pollution, even smoky atmospheres. It is also wind-resistant, regenerates well after light cutting back, and grows in sun or light shade.

GROWTH HABIT A medium-sized tree, reaching up to 15m/50ft, with a compact, densely leafy round crown.

PROPAGATION Propagation is best achieved by gathering fruits, storing then in polythene bags until they rot, then cleaning them and sowing them in containers. Germination can be erratic. Seedlings are best pricked out into small pots of compost before potting on or planting in nursery beds and growing on for a further season. If the plants get individual care, they may be planted in permanent sites at the end of their second season.

ROLE IN LANDSCAPE Whitebeam comes into flower before hawthorn. It is mostly found in light woodland and scrub, mainly on chalk and limestone in the southern third of England. In Scotland it normally occurs as a single tree on the edge of a wood or in a hedgerow, but is less common than the rowan. Sometimes it grows in scattered localities elsewhere, such as on inland cliffs. There are many different microspecies of whitebeam in England (including the rock whitebeam in Derbyshire), some of which are extremely rare and restricted in range.

TRUNK, BARK AND BRANCHES The trunk divides into two or more major branches which are steeply angled; the bark is smooth and light grey; the shoots are downy.

LEAVES As the oval leaves unfold in late April they form upright, goblet-shaped groups, glistening white from the felted hairs on the undersides. Once mature they vary in shape and are up to around 12cm/5in long, shiny green above with white hairs below, with many pairs of veins and usually finely toothed margins. They turn yellow and pale brown before falling in autumn.

BUDS, FLOWERS AND FRUIT In May and June, loose clusters of five-petalled, creamy-white flowers appear in broad, flattened heads. These develop into round or oblong fruits, orange to scarlet, spotted with pores.

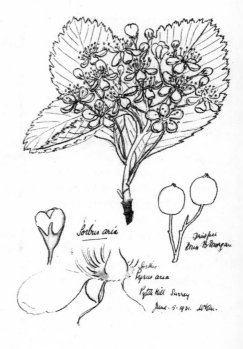

PLANT–ANIMAL RELATIONSHIPS The tree is visited by a wide range of insects, including tortricoid moths whose larvae eat the leaves, which may also be tunnelled by leaf miners and blistered by gall mites. The big berries are enjoyed by larger birds in early winter, and often eaten in preference to any other berry.

HISTORICAL AND OTHER USES A pioneer species tolerant of maritime conditions, whitebeam was often used for the stabilisation of soil, as well as by herbalists and pharmacists.

NAME The common name is derived from Saxon *Weissbaum*, white tree.

OTHER SPECIES, often quite rare, include *S. bristoliensis*, *S. devoniensis*, *S. bristoliensis*, *S. eminens*, *S. lancastriensis*, *S. porrigentiformis*, *S. subcuneata*, *S. vexans*, *S. wilmottiana* and rock whitebeam (*S. rupicola*).

Sorbus aucuparia (Rosaceae)

ROWAN, MOUNTAIN ASH

Lest witches should obtain the power,
Of Hawkie's milk in evil hour,
She winds a red thread round her horn,
And milks thro' row'n tree night and morn:
Against the blink of evil eye
She knows each antidote to play.
    'Folk Lore', James Napier (1879)

This graceful, small tree with its smooth bark and eye-catching foliage, flowers and fruit has long been a favourite in cultivation. The hardy and graceful rowan is not only ornamental, but wind-resistant and tolerant of air pollution, so is often grown in town gardens and as a street tree. Moderate in size, it never casts too much shade so other plants can grow under it; it is sometimes coppiced. As it grows quickly in its first five years, foresters sometimes use it as a 'nurse' tree to give shelter to young oaks and other slower-growing trees. Rowan prefers a sunny, open position but will grow in semi-shade. Although it likes a free-draining, moist but not marshy soil, preferably neutral to acid, it will grow on sandstone or calcareous soils.

GROWTH HABIT Reaching 2.5–2.75m/8–9ft in the first five years, it is normally no more than 4m/13ft at maturity, when it spreads out into a loosely branching head.

PROPAGATION Rowan is best propagated from seed by gathering berries just before they ripen and storing them in polythene bags until they rot. They should then be washed and the seeds sown in moist sand; some will germinate the following spring, others may stay dormant for a further year. Thin out, grow on and transplant to 1m/39in apart, planting in the final position two years later.

ROLE IN LANDSCAPE Rowan grows in woodland, moors and scrub on light, free-draining soils throughout most of the British Isles (in Ireland it has been introduced). The sight of it loaded with clusters of red berries on moorland slopes and roadsides is spectacular in the Highlands of Scotland. It is particularly widespread on rocky ground, sometimes appearing to balance on a bare ledge of sandstone or limestone.

TRUNK, BARK AND BRANCHES It has grey bark, ringed with pores. Greyish-brown twig-like branches in winter carry large brown buds covered with white hairs.

LEAVES The compound-pinnate leaves have five to seven pairs of slender, oblong leaflets and a terminal leaflet, each up to 6cm/2½in long, sharply toothed, deep-green above and grey-green below. They usually turn yellowish and red before decaying to brown in the autumn.

BUDS, FLOWERS AND FRUIT In May and June it produces fragrant white blossoms and in October a profusion of scarlet berries. Along with the whitebeam and service-tree, the rowan is classified in a sub-genus of the rose family Rosaceae, *Sorbus*, which has apple-like fruits and small white flowers in branched clusters. Rowan's dense, flat-topped creamy-white flowers (up to 15cm/6in across) have an unpleasant scent and are followed by bunches of juicy berries which ripen from yellow to orange and finally scarlet by September.

PLANT–ANIMAL RELATIONSHIPS Rowan's clusters of heavily scented flowers attract flies, bees and beetles to the abundant nectar and pollen. The bright orange-yellow berries provide winter food for larger birds, especially members of the thrush family, and innumerable finches – they peck at the flesh of the fruit, leaving the core on the tree.

HISTORICAL AND OTHER USES Rowan wood is strong, flexible and yellow-grey in colour. It was once widely used for making small carved objects, tool handles and, along with yew, longbows. The berries were also used as bait in traps to catch thrushes, redwings and field-fares. People, too, enjoyed the fruit when made into a drink; John Evelyn, in *Sylva*, described 'an incomparable drink, familiar in Wales'. The tree was coppiced to provide wood for poles and hoops, and some of the bark was used in tanning. There was a belief that a rowan tree in a field protected cattle from being struck by lightning, and bunches of rowan twigs used to be nailed to cattle shelters to protect them from witches. Rowan berries, which have a sharp tang, are added to windfall apples and made into a jelly used as an accompaniment to game.

NAME Latin *aucuparia* from *auceps*, fowler, referring to the way that bird-catchers used the plant as bait. Virgil wrote that rowan trees attracted thrushes. The common name comes from the old *runer*, to know, a word connected with runes and magic; mountain ash refers to the high altitudes where it grows, especially in the Highlands.

Sorbus torminalis (Rosaceae)

WILD SERVICE-TREE

Budding, the service tree, white
Almost as whitebeam, threw,
From the under of leaf upright,
Flecks like a showering snow
On the flame-shaped junipers green,
On the sombre mounds of the yew.
Like silvery tapers bright
By a solemn cathedral screen,
They glistened to closer view
   'A Faith on Trial', George Meredith (1828–1909)

This beautiful deciduous shrub or small tree, strongly associated with the ancient woodlands of Britain, is now very rare. If you can obtain one, it can be grown as an ornamental specimen in a large garden, as in the walled garden at the Bishop's Palace, Fulham, London. With a broad, domed head and attractive shape, it has much to recommend it. It thrives in sun or semi-shade and moist but well-drained soils, although it fruits and flowers best in sun and grows on almost any kind of soil provided it is not too impoverished. It should be planted where its attractive shape, leaves, flowers and foliage can readily be seen. At first glance its leaves resemble maple, and its flowers and fruit rowan, so it can be misidentified.

GROWTH HABIT It takes decades to reach halfway to its maximum height. Usually it is a medium sized tree, well below its potential of 15–23m/50–75ft. As it grows towards the light, in woodland it tends to be a narrowish tree, but in more open positions it spreads out more widely.

PROPAGATION It reproduces itself mainly from the roots, but seed is produced each autumn in edible fruits. These can be handled in a similar way to whitebeam. Germination, though, is variable; it often does not germinate freely and new plants grow quite slowly, which contributes to its poor distribution.

ROLE IN LANDSCAPE Wild service-trees are an indicator of ancient woodland. Their distribution is limited and almost confined to clay soils, particularly where there is underlying chalk, in ancient woods south of a line joining the Humber and Dee estuaries, mainly in the south-east. Towards its northern limits in England it also grows on limestone. It is a long-lived, hardy tree and also, occasionally, found in hedgerows.

TRUNK, BARK AND BRANCHES The bark, which is similar to hawthorn, is dark grey, smooth at first but becoming broken and lightly fissured so that it peels in rectangular strips.

LEAVES Deep-green, shiny, lobed leaves begin to appear in the middle of May. In autumn they turn a wonderful deep orange.

BUDS, FLOWERS AND FRUIT Clear green buds open in late April to early May, followed by open clusters of white flowers in May and June, then brown oval fruits up to 1.6cm/¾in long. The sprays of white flowers with yellow stamens appear at the end of the twigs in large bunches, eventually developing into hard green speckled berries, shiny above and slightly downy below, which can turn brownish red in autumn. They are something like hawthorn berries, but larger. When they ripen in September they have numerous large but inconspicuous rough pores.

PLANT–ANIMAL RELATIONSHIPS Pollinating flies are attracted to the nectar; the seeds are often attacked by the grubs of a seed wasp; the whole fruits, which have a prune-like flavour, are relished by birds, mice and other wildlife; the flowers and leaves also attract a wide range of insects, including some rare moths.

HISTORICAL AND OTHER USES The acid-tasting berries were used to make jams and liqueurs, and called 'chequers' in Kent. From Roman times they were used medicinally.

NAME Latin *torminalis,* of or relating to the gripes – a rather unfair description as the fruit, although acid, is no more likely to give pains when eaten than any other sour fruit.

OTHER SPECIES The rare true service-tree (*Sorbus domestica*) was first found in the Wyre Forest and reported by Alderman Pitts of Worcester in a letter published in *The Philosophical Transactions of the Royal Society*, 1678. Although it grows extensively in southern Europe, no other examples of this species were found in the British Isles until two were identified on two Glamorgan cliffs in 1983, and more later in Gloucestershire. The main method of seed dispersal is via birds, and the Glamorgan and Gloucestershire sites are less than 100 km/60 miles from Wyre Forest, making a direct link very likely.

Taxus baccata (Taxaceae)

YEW

Beneath those rugged elms, that yew-tree's shade
Where heaves the turf in many a mouldering heap,
Each in his narrow cell for ever laid,
The rude forefathers of the hamlet sleep.
'Elegy Written in a Country Church-Yard', Thomas Gray (1716–71)

Whether young or old, yew, with its dense, sombre, dark green foliage and broad, pyramidal shape, is Britain's most impressive evergreen tree. A really old yew tree can stay green for over a thousand years. Yew can be a fine specimen tree in a larger garden, assuming the shape of a conical bush in early life, but is often grown as a hedge. Dense and compact throughout the year, its dark green colour acts as a foil for the bright hues of herbaceous plants. In a congenial site yew can, after its early years, grow surprisingly fast. Resistant to pollution, it is excellent in urban gardens and inner city parks. It also has the advantage of growing in sun or deep shade in any well-drained soil from acid to alkaline, but does like some moisture in the ground in winter. A light covering of straw should be spread around young plants, which are likely to suffer from frosts. While trees can be trimmed in summer or early autumn, old, over-grown hedges will regenerate well if cut back hard in the spring.

At Sissinghurst in the Weald of Kent, Vita Sackville-West used yew, together with brick walls, to divide the gardens into 'rooms'. At Powis Castle, Welshpool, Powys, the massive buttresses of yew are 9.1m/30ft high. In his garden in Herefordshire, Sir Roy Strong has created a spectacular topiary garden of yews on symmetrical lines. Unusually, yew thrives in shade. When surrounded and overhung by taller trees, it becomes more dense and compact.

All parts of yew except the fleshy berries contain toxic alkaloids which are particularly poisonous. Livestock sometimes eat small branches or clippings, but the smallest amount proves fatal, so yew should never be grown on land where horses or other domesticated animals might graze. Deer, however, are said to be able to eat it with impunity. Some of the oldest yew trees in England grow in churchyards because these, being sacred grounds, were always walled even when there were far fewer hedges and fences prior to the Enclosure Acts. In order to grow enough

yew to supply bows and arrows, the trees were therefore planted where stock could not get at them.

GROWTH HABIT Yew is remarkable for its slow growth. Even ten-year-old plants are often only 1m/36in in height. Massive but never very tall, yew can be low and bushy or a tree up to 20m/70ft with a rounded crown.

PROPAGATION In the wild, yew pollen is distributed by the wind, in 'faithful cloud and living smoke' (Tennyson). Yew can also be raised from seeds in the berries, which ripen in autumn. Once collected, they need to be cleared, by washing, from the pulp of the epimatium (the aril-like outgrowth of the ovary) in which they are encased. Patience is needed as they can take up to two years to germinate and the crop comes up irregularly. They are then best lined out 30cm/1ft apart and grown for a further two years before planting permanently in autumn or spring. Yew can also be propagated from cuttings taken with a heel in autumn and grown in a cold frame – care must be taken not to damage the brittle roots when handling.

ROLE IN LANDSCAPE Widespread in woodland and scrub on chalk and limestone in the south and west of England, but absent from East Anglia

and the east Midlands, yew is often associated with churches, where splendid old trees still thrive. It still grows wild in a few areas in the Lake District and on the chalk downs of the south, especially in Surrey and Sussex – one of the finest yew woods in Europe is in the Kingley Vale National Nature Reserve near Chichester, Sussex. The most ancient yew in Britain, estimated to be around 5,000 years old, is at Fortingall churchyard, near Perth and Kinross. Yew is extremely hardy and many examples live for over 500 years, although the age of individual trees is often unclear because in churchyards their roots could be cut during gravedigging, inhibiting growth.

TRUNK, BARK AND BRANCHES The often massive, reddish-brown bark is fluted; it is soft and flaking and peels continuously, giving the trunk a patchy appearance. It becomes greyer and deeply furrowed with age. Lower branches of old trees often rest on the ground.

LEAVES Tough green shoots are spirally set with strap-like needles – dull green-yellow on the underside, glossy dark green and shiny on the top, each up to 2.5cm/1in long.

BUDS, FLOWERS AND FRUIT Male and female flowers, which open in February and March, are usually borne on separate trees but can sometimes occur on the same tree. Both appear from the leaf axils on the undersides of twigs, the small, round, yellow male flowers releasing clouds of pollen and the tiny, acorn-like, yellowish-green females swelling to form the fruit. Female flowers can be distinguished by their minute green embryo berries, swelling into fleshy, translucent epimatium or red pulp. The hard, poisonous, olive-green seed is surrounded, apart from a hole at the top, by the non-poisonous epimatium which becomes sweet and red in August and September.

PLANT–ANIMAL RELATIONSHIPS Berries ripen in August, and the arils turn red by September and are sought after by greenfinches and mistle thrushes. Young branches are dangerous to animals as the seeds are poisonous. But the seed cups surrounding them are not poisonous to birds and many, including song thrushes, blackbirds and jays, eagerly consume them. Birds also make nest sites in the dense canopy, which gives them cover throughout year. Yew pollen is eaten by early-flying honey-bees.

HISTORICAL AND OTHER USES Evidence of the existence of yew has been found at excavated Bronze Age sites. Longbows and arrows made from yew were prized by the yeomen of England and used with stunning success. The conquest of Ireland by Henry II in 1172 was said to have been due to the skill of English archers – who boasted that none but an Englishman could bend that powerful weapon, the yew bow. It was also used with considerable success at Crécy, Poitiers and Agincourt. In the fifth year of the reign of Edward IV, every man in England was ordered to keep a bow, in length equal to his own height, made of yew, wych-hazel, ash or awlune (laburnum). Such was the demand for yew through-out Europe for weapons that each tree was protected; in Venice a law was enacted that every ship arriving in the port had to bring ten yew staves with every butt of Malmsey wine. In ancient Welsh law the consecrated yew of the monks supplanted in value the sacred mistletoe of the Druids. Yew is still prized for fine furniture, sculpture and turned articles such as bowls, and planted in labyrinths or mazes, like the one at Hampton Court Palace. Since the early 1990s, yew clippings have been used by the phar-maceuticals industry in the manufacture of the cancer drug, Taxol.

NAME The common name is derived from Old English *iw, eow,* said to be the oldest tree name in the Indo-European languages. The word has many religious associations, both Christian and pagan.

Tilia cordata (Tiliaceae)

SMALL-LEAVED LIME

Well, they are gone, and here must I remain,
This lime-tree bower my prison! I have lost
Beauties and feelings, such as would have been
Most sweet to my remembrance even when age
Had dimmed mine eyes to blindness!
  'This Lime-Tree Bower My Prison', Samuel Taylor Coleridge (1772–1834)

This tall, graceful, long-lived, deciduous tree is recognised by its neat, rounded-to-heart-shaped, leathery leaves and nectar-rich flowers in June which are so visited by bees that the tree virtually hums with the sound of them. Spectacular, slow-growing and spreading, lime responds well to pollarding or coppicing so it can be pruned to keep it below maximum height and grown in a variety of places. In large gardens and parks it is often planted to make a stately avenue. One drawback for some is that the leaves attract aphids that produce sticky honeydew which drips on to whatever is below (especially parked cars). Lime is frost-hardy and grows well in sun or semi-shade and fertile, moist but well-drained soil, preferably alkaline to neutral. It likes plenty of water in dry periods. Ancient examples of small-leaved lime planted 350 years ago by Charles I can be found at Hampton Court Palace.

GROWTH HABIT Maximum height is 30m/98ft.

PROPAGATION It is best propagated by collecting seed and sowing thickly in boxes of seed compost, then leaving for a year and planting out the seedlings 30cm/1ft apart in a nursery bed. They can be transplanted up to two years later, growing on for a further one or two years. If only a few plants are required, seedlings can be pricked out into small pots initially, then grown on in three-litre pots for planting out in their third season. When young, even relatively large trees can be transplanted in the winter. A mature tree throws up a continuous and thickly growing 'belt' of suckers from the base which are best cut back.

ROLE IN LANDSCAPE Small-leaved lime is quite rare. It is found scattered in woods throughout lowland England, but is more to be seen on deep, base-rich soils in central England and Essex. It is planted as a roadside or street tree, especially in avenues, as it withstands regular heavy pruning and atmospheric pollution. One of the best known lime avenues is on the Backs at Trinity College, Cambridge. At Chatsworth, Derbyshire, the pleached limes are spectacular, as they are at Sissinghurst, Kent. Other large collections are at Bushey Park and the Clumber Estate, Nottinghamshire. It is not found in Ireland.

TRUNK, BARK AND BRANCHES The usually upright, thick buttressed trunk has smooth, grey bark which may later become ribbed. It is so strong that its fibre was once used in the manufacture of rope.

LEAVES Smaller than the leaves of most other limes, the dark green leaves are hairless except for a few orange-brown tufts in the vein-axils; they are up to 9cm/3½in long, toothed and heart-shaped, tapering abruptly to a fine tip.

BUDS, FLOWERS AND FRUIT The small, fragrant, cup-shaped, yellow-white, five-petalled flowers appear in June and July and are arranged in starry clusters on long, obliquely upright stalks, but they do not appear until a tree is about 40 years old at the earliest. When they open they have a rich and invigorating scent. As in all linden species, both the flower and seed clusters are attached to a wing-like bract like a little 'aeroplane propellor' which helps in the wind dispersal of the seeds. The short-beaked fruits which ripen in October are smooth and rounded.

PLANT–ANIMAL RELATIONSHIPS In summer the trees hum with the sound of myriad bees attracted by the nectar-filled flowers; honey bees pollinate lime and can be observed clinging to the stamens and stigmas. Many other insects also feed on the sugary honeydew produced by aphids. Birds are attracted to the array of insects it supports. The leaves are food for buff-tip and lime hawk-moth caterpillars; the small, round, hard green berries are eaten by a variety of animals.

HISTORICAL AND OTHER USES Lime is one of the softest native hardwoods; it cuts cleanly and does not warp after seasoning. It has long been valued for sounding boards, the keys for pianos and organs, for carving and model making. The Romans used lime wood for agricultural implements and shields, while the bark was prized as a writing material and for making head-dresses. In England it was carved into intricate patterns – examples include finely carved friezes by Grinling Gibbons (1648–1721) at Windsor Castle; the ceiling at Petworth; the choir of St Paul's Cathedral, London; St Paul's Church, Covent Garden, and Trinity College, Cambridge. As lime floats well it was also dug out to make canoes. Until the eighteenth century the inner fibre of lime coppice poles was stripped and made into rope in Gloucester, Devon and Cornwall. Honey made from lime flowers is especially prized in Europe. The flowers and bracts are still collected, dried and stored in tightly closed containers for medicinal use as a soporific, usually in the form of linden tea. Long ago lime shoots were used as winter food.

NAME Latin *cordata* refers to the heart-shaped leaves.

OTHER SPECIES Large-leaved lime (*T. platyphyllos*) is tall, up to 32m/105ft, and now extremely rare as a wild tree. It is still found in the Wye Valley where, in places, lime, elm and oak share dominance with beech. Even though there is a dispute as to whether *T. platyphyllos* is native or an early pre-Roman introduction, it is included in the list of British native plants issued by the Institute of Terrestrial Ecology at Monks Wood (the centre for biological and distribution records in Britain). The much-used street tree, European linden (*T. × europaea*), is a natural hybrid between *T. cordata* and *T. platyphyllos* and seldom included among native species; the most famous example is Unter den Linden in East Berlin.

Ulex europaeus (Fabaceae)

GORSE, FURZE, WHIN

Love you not, then, to list and hear
The crackling of the gorse-flower near,
Pouring an orange-scented tide
Of fragrance o'er the desert wide?
　'A June Day', William Howitt (1792–1879)

When this dense, prickly, dark-green shrub breaks into flower in spring, it fills large patches of the countryside with a breathtaking blaze of brilliant yellow as each plant is smothered with bright flowers. Unlike the smooth stems of broom which also has spectacular yellow flowers, gorse is spiny. A nice-looking and hardy shrub, gorse enriches the soil's fertility by adding nitrogen gleaned from the air. It likes full sun and will grow in most well-drained soils, tolerating even the poorest and driest, but it has a preference for acid to neutral soils. Strong and wind-resistant, it is particularly useful for coastal gardens and exposed sites, but may be damaged by frost, although it will regenerate. Since it looks its best when young and does not respond well to pruning, plants are often replaced when stems begin to die back. Like other members of the pea family, gorse pods split and twist when ripe, thrusting out seeds with amazing force in all directions. In the early nineteenth century, William Cobbett praised gorse as being 'sweet-smelling, an abundant flowerer, and evergreen. It should be in every shrubbery, and it does not disgrace a border even'. But gorse has been displaced in gardens by *Forsythia*, introduced from across the Atlantic. Despite its toughness, gorse is now seldom planted in borders or grown as a thick, intruder-proof hedge.

GROWTH HABIT Upright or bushy and rounded, it grows up to 2.5m/8ft with an intricate arrangement of strong, deeply grooved spines and small, stiff leaves.

PROPAGATION Gorse is easily raised from seed sown in a cold frame soon after ripening, with two to three seedlings grown on in a pot. The strongest seedling should be planted out the following autumn. Semi-ripe cuttings with a heel can be taken in summer and planted out the following autumn or spring.

ROLE IN LANDSCAPE Gorse grows in rough grassland, heaths, open woods and dunes, often on sandy or peaty soils throughout the British Isles, ascending to 500m/1,650ft in the Pennines. It is frequently confused with the closely related western gorse (*Ulex gallii*) and dwarf gorse (*Ulex minor*), which occupy similar habitats.

TRUNK AND BARK The densely spiny, spreading branches form thickets of impenetrable scrub – from a distance they look like spiny leaves.

LEAVES The leaves are in groups of three in young plants and reduced to scales or weak spines on older shrubs.

BUDS, FLOWERS AND FRUIT Abundant deep yellow pea-flowers, up to 1.8cm/¾in long, appear singly or in small clusters from March to June, although in mild conditions gorse can bloom for much longer. The flowers have a strange coconut-like scent. Popping sounds can be heard from the bush on warm summer days when the hairy, blackish-brown, 1.5cm/½in-long seed pods burst open to eject shiny seeds up to 6m/20ft away. The old country saying, 'When gorse is out of blossom, then kissing's out of fashion!' indicates that there is never a day in the year in the south of England and Ireland without a gorse flower somewhere.

PLANT–ANIMAL RELATIONSHIPS Gorse's rich-scented flowers attract honey-bees and bumble- bees to the pollen, and the thorns are food for caterpillars of the green hairstreak butterfly. The dense growth is excellent cover for small birds and the prickles protect their nest sites. It also provides nesting sites for linnets.

HISTORICAL AND OTHER USES There are records of gorse wood and gorse charcoal from Neolithic times in Britain, and it was put to many domestic uses. Because it ignites quickly, it was used for starting fires and was also used for cleaning chimneys and tilling the soil. In some places, at midsummer, blazing branches were carried round the cow herd to bring them health. When ground up, gorse is sometimes still used as a nitrogen-rich fodder for cattle. A yellow dye is obtained from the bark, flowers and young shoots.

NAME Latin *Ulex* from Celtic *ec* or *oc*, prickle or sharp point. The common name furze is from Old English *fyrs*, from *fyrh*, *furh*, fir tree. The name furze is used in the south, gorse in the north and whin in the east.

OTHER SPECIES The similar but smaller western gorse (*Ulex gallii*) and dwarf gorse (*Ulex minor*).

Ulmus glabra (Ulmaceae)

MOUNTAIN ELM, WYCH ELM

And the plane to the pine-tree is whispering some tale of love
Till it rustles with laughter and tosses its mantle of green,
And the gloom of the wych-elm's hollow is lit with the iris sheen
Of the burnished rainbow throat and the silver breast of a dove.
  'Magdalen Walks', Oscar Wilde (1854–1900)

A typical hedgerow tree, wych elm looks its best in spring when the blossoms appear in April, just before the leaves expand. A number of species of elm grow in Britain, but wych elm, an attractive small or medium sized tree, is the sole undisputed native. It can be found in most parts of Britain and seeds itself abundantly in the right conditions. In Scotland, it was often known as a tree of the glens and occurs wild in many areas, especially in the lowlands where on good sites it forms a large tree. It endures a greater degree of smoke and pollution than other elms. Like other elm species in Britain, it was affected by the devastating fungus that caused Dutch elm disease in the mid 1960s, but it withstood attacks more tenaciously – many trees resisted or recovered more than other elm species. A large number survived in Scotland, and in Abbots Ripton, Huntingdon, and St Mary's, Scilly. There are three examples at Parson's Green on New King's Road, Fulham, London.

GROWTH HABIT Its maximum height is usually about 15m/50ft, but it is sometimes larger. Stagnant water near the surface of the soil enfeebles growth and causes lichen to appear on the bark.

PROPAGATION It does not yield suckers like the English elm but produces seed freely. The seeds are usually ripe about the middle of June when they should be gathered and immediately sown. Germination is varied; at least half the seeds will be infertile.

ROLE IN LANDSCAPE This elm is much slower in growth and has a shorter bole than the English elm, but it is more spreading in habit and, according to many, a much more picturesque tree.

TRUNK, BARK AND BRANCHES Its fan-like branches terminate in robust twigs; the distinctive bark is silver-grey and smooth, eventually fissured and brownish.

LEAVES The large, dull green leaves, up to 10cm/4in long, are simple, entire with a serrated edge, rounded to elliptical, rough and hairy above, and often uneven at the base. Wych elm, like other elms and hazel, is distinguishable by the asymmetric base to its leaves.

BUDS, FLOWERS AND FRUIT The flowers are petalless, forming rounded masses of conspicuous red stamens. These are followed by pale green, oval, winged fruits, each with a central seed, which are dispersed in June.

PLANT–ANIMAL RELATIONSHIPS Wych elm is host to several important species of lichens, mosses and invertebrates, on which birds and bats depend. It also provides nest and roost sites and, according to the Cornish

Wildlife Trust, it supports white hairstreak, comma and large tortoise-shell butterflies. In Scotland, only a few old species are known to be host to the very rare orange-fruited elm lichen *Caloplaca luteoalba* and the lichen *Baccidia incompta*; the latter is found only on wych elms at Haddo, north-east Scotland.

HISTORICAL AND OTHER USES Although the timber is not bracketed in the same category as English elm, it is durable and was once used for many agricultural purposes, such as the handles of spades, forks, etc. It was often made into bows and riding-switches – as well as drains, along with English elm (some Roman examples have been excavated in the City of London). It is still used for planking, baulks, some furniture, coffins and flooring.

NAME Old English *wych*, pliable, referring to the twigs.

Ulmus procera (Ulmaceae)
ELM

Oh! as I trace again thy winding hill,
Mine eyes admire, my heart adores thee still,
Thou drooping Elm! beneath whose boughs I lay,
And frequent mus'd the twilight hours away
    'Lines Written beneath an Elm in the Churchyard of Harrow',
    Lord Byron (1788–1824)

Until Dutch elm disease was introduced in the late 1960s, few trees rivalled the vigour, stability and beauty of the elm in England. John Constable immortalised elms in his paintings, especially *The Hay Wain* (1821), in which he painted every crack and crevice of the bark, showing them branching near the base with a spreading, dome-shaped outline. The disease – a wilt fungus, *Ophiostoma ulmi*, spread by the bark beetles *Scolytus scolytus* and *Scolytus multistriatus* which feed on young twigs – wiped out the stately canopies of English elms that once were part of the countryside. The fungus clogs the tree's circulatory system, blocking the flow of sap until the branches wilt and die, one by one; eventually the roots also die, starved of nutrients from the leaves. First recorded in the nineteenth century, the disease was was a concern as early as 1927, and rapidly spread across southern England in the late 1960s and early 1970s, destroying millions of trees and changing the English landscape forever. According to the UK Forestry Commission, by the 1990s over 25 million of the 30 million elm trees in the UK had been killed by the disease. In many parks, the fallen trees have been left as standing deadwood to provide for fungi, insects and hole nesting birds that rely on dead and decaying timber.

The bark beetles feed first on the upper branches of a tree, introducing the fungal spores to exposed tissue; if a tree is not allowed to grow any higher than 4.5m/15ft it is seldom infected. The beetle also seems not to be a threat to trees under 15 years old. Attempts to eliminate the bark beetle with insecticide is both ineffective and bad for the environment.

GROWTH HABIT In ideal, open, low-lying situations, elm occasionally used to reach a height of 18–30m/60–98ft, but usually less. During the first ten years it can reach 7.5–9m/25–30ft. Before Dutch elm disease, the age and size of elms approached that of oaks.

PROPAGATION Mostly propagated by root-suckers from old trees, or by layers from stools. Often, not all the roots of old diseased trees die and they may later produce unexpected small suckers which grow into small trees. These, however, like their parents, may succumb to the disease after about 15 years.

ROLE IN LANDSCAPE Elm was once widely found in woods and hedgerows, especially in the southern part of Britain and on almost all soils, preferring a rich loam. Because of the variety of species and subspecies, trees can be notoriously difficult to identify. In the Domesday Book at least 40 places were listed with names derived from the elm.

TRUNK, BARK AND BRANCHES The branches are numerous and spreading, the bark rugged.

LEAVES Leaves are alternate, ovate, rough, doubly toothed (the uneven edges, or teeth, also have little teeth) and slightly uneven near the stalk.

BUDS, FLOWERS AND FRUIT In March and April before the leaves come, flowers appear forming rounded masses of conspicuous stamens. The pale green winged fruits develop quickly, each with a single brown seed.

PLANT–ANIMAL RELATIONSHIPS A wide variety of insects are attracted to elm and the tiny wind-dispersed winged seeds are readily eaten by birds and small mammals.

HISTORICAL AND OTHER USES As the wood is strong and easily shaped, it was used to make furniture including chair frames, wheels, doors, wheelbarrows and coffins. In water it lasts longer than most other woods; in many ancient cities, hollowed elms were used as water-pipes as well as in barge- and boat-building. It is still used for work boats in wet dock.

NAME The root of the common name is probably from Old Icelandic *álmr*, although some sources consider both elm and the generic name *Ulmus* are derived from the Saxon *elm* or *ulm*. A similar name runs through all the Celtic languages.

OTHER SPECIES *Ulmus minor* and plot's elm (*Ulmus plotii*).

Vaccinium myrtillus (Ericaceae)

BILBERRY, BLAEBERRY

A low-growing deciduous shrub of woodland and acid heath, it grows to knee- or thigh-height, has small, pinkish-white, waxy, globular flowers followed by fine violet-blue berries with a light silvery surface bloom. Preferring well-drained, preferably sloping, ground in well-mulched acidic soil, like its cousins the cranberry and whortleberry it is abundant on hill slopes and higher heathland. Dominant in northern pinewoods and high altitudes, especially in Scotland, it likes moist soil and does not tolerate drought. It can tolerate strong winds but not maritime exposure. It is very reliant on the correct amount of light. The Royal Society for the Protection of Birds has carried out extensive research on this shrub because of the wildlife reliant on it: 'in dense woodland with little light, blaeberry dies. It seems to grow best (out-competing heather) where there is a moderate level of light.'

ROLE IN LANDSCAPE Although closely associated with Scotland, bilberry was chosen by Leeds as its favourite wild flower in a nationwide vote organised by the conservation charity, Plantlife International. In most upland oakwoods, bluebells (*Hyacinthoides non-scriptus*), brambles (*Rubus* spp.) and ferns tend to be most common where the soil is relatively rich, with heather (*Calluna vulgaris*), bilberries and mosses becoming more prominent on soils that are acid and deficient in nutrients.

PROPAGATION To produce fruit and seed bilberry needs to be cross-pollinated by insects. Ripe seeds should be collected in July and August and sown in a greenhouse in a lime-free potting mix just covering them. Once they are about 5cm/2in tall, transfer the seedlings into largish potswhere they should remain (they do not like root disturbance) until they are put out in their permanent position. They are usually kept in a lightly shaded position in a greenhouse for at least their first winter.

GROWTH HABIT A creeping shrub about 60cm/24in maximum in size.

TRUNK, BARK AND BRANCHES Twigs are three-angled and green.

LEAVES Clear, bright green, deciduous leaves that redden into autumn foliage.

BUDS, FLOWERS AND FRUIT Its hermaphrodite flowers are in bloom from April to June and are pollinated by insects including bees, flies, moths and butterflies. The aromatic, highly coloured berries contain seeds that ripen from about July to September.

PLANT–ANIMAL RELATIONSHIPS Bilberry is noted for attracting wildlife and is the foodplant of moth caterpillars including the arran carpet, beautiful snout, marbled carpet and common pug. In 2000, bilberry became part of a Regional Action Plan for the Highland and Western Isles by Butterfly Conservation because it is needed by the german cousin moth (*Paradiarsia sobrina*). Its larvae feed initially on bilberry or heather before they switch to birch to complete their development. The berries are much sought after by deer and birds. The RSPB stresses that bilberry is an important foodplant for the capercaillie: 'Fully-grown birds eat the leaves in summer and berries in autumn, and the chicks eat moth caterpillars that themselves eat blaeberry leaves.'

HISTORICAL AND OTHER USES A range of dyes – purple, blue, violet, brown, green – was produced by the bilberry in Scotland, including the Outer Hebrides, some of which were used in tartans and tweeds. The berries are too sharp for some tastes when raw, but delicious when cooked with a little sugar, or made into preserves, a cool drink or a hot tea. Bilberry tarts and jellies laced with whisky were traditional Highland treats. The fruit has purported medicinal properties: British Air force pilots ate bilberry jam as it was thought to improve eyesight. It is the plant badge of the clans of Buchanan, Comyn or Cumming, Dundas, Louchbuie, MacLaine, MacNab and Scott.

NAME *Vaccinium* is thought to be from a Scandinavian word of unknown meaning. The common name comes from Old English *blae*, blue-black. It is known as *lus an deare* in Gaelic.

OTHER SPECIES

CRANBERRY *Vaccinium oxycoccos*

A low-growing and creeping evergreen shrub with sparse tiny leaves and prostrate stems that root at intervals, cranberry is often found in damp boggy areas of Scottish moorland or on heathland if it is wet enough, in most parts of Scotland including some of the islands, but is very local in distribution. Its delightful small flowers – deep pink, drooping with upturned petals – are sometimes difficult to spot among other vegetation. The fruit is edible and normally red but can be spotted with brown. Cranberry grows in most soils and will tolerate slightly acidic (peaty) conditions, as long as they are damp enough. It is very suitable for rockeries, low borders and tubs. It is the plant badge of the Cameron and MacFarlane clans.

COWBERRY *Vaccinium vitis-idea*

Cowberry, found mostly in Scotland, is an important part of the plant communities in mountains, moorland and woods where it provides cover for ground-nesting birds. The fruit is eaten in early autumn. A low-growing evergreen shrub with small bell-like flowers, white suffused with pink, that droop from the ends of its short stems, it adapts well to gardens. Due to its underground creeping stems, in some places it is often the dominant species. Like so many native plants, cowberry is difficult to obtain. It tolerates damp and acidic soils and enhances rockeries, borders or tubs. It is the plant badge of the Chattan, Davidson, MacGilivray, MacLeod of the Lewes, MacPherson and MacQueen clans.

Also: the small cranberry (*V. microcarpum*) and bog bilberry (*V. uliginosum*), the latter very local to northern England and southern Scotland.

Viburnum lantana (Caprifoliaceae)

WAYFARING-TREE

Wayfaring tree! What ancient claim
Hast thou to that right pleasant name?
Was it that some faint pilgrim came
Unhopedly to thee?
  'The Forest Minstrels and Other Poems' (1821),
  William Howitt (1792–1879)

This dainty small tree or shrub is common in hedgerows in the south of England. It is distinguished by conspicuous berries in autumn, varying in colour according to the time of year from red to black. With its thick, soft, almost velvety leaves and clusters of fragrant white flowers, the wayfaring-tree provides colour and interest throughout the growing season in shrub borders, woodland corners or as a free-standing tree. A member of the honeysuckle family, it is found on limy soils and is not difficult to cultivate. The most noticeable features of this appealing tree is its softness: its twigs and buds are felted with greyish hairs, the stems pliant and the underside of the rounded leaves covered by dense, white, silky hairs, giving the whole plant a dusty appearance. It is easily maintained, growing in sun or semi-shade in well-drained soils, preferably alkaline clays; it tolerates dry conditions but dislikes smoky atmospheres.

GROWTH HABIT The wayfaring-tree can grow to 6m/20ft maximum if left untrimmed, but seldom reaches more than 4m/13ft. It is light-demanding, and does not grow tall under the canopy of other trees.

PROPAGATION Fruits should be gathered as they turn black, stratified, then sown in early spring in a cold frame. Later, thin the seedlings and leave until autumn before setting out 30cm/1ft apart. Grow on for one or two years before planting out permanently. Cuttings with a heel may be taken in late summer and potted after rooting.

ROLE IN LANDSCAPE The wayfaring-tree is native in woodland, scrub and hedges, especially on base-rich soils throughout the southern half of Britain in a line south of Glamorgan to South Lincolnshire. A characteristic feature of downlands and bushy places on chalk and limestone in central and southern England, in other places it has been introduced as a hedgerow and roadside tree. It regrows well after hard cutting or trimming, but its growth is too open for a stockproof hedge.

TRUNK, BARK AND BRANCHES Thin branches are pliant and the grey-brown bark is marked with leaf scars on the older growth.

LEAVES The opposite pairs of thick, ovate, regularly toothed leaves are opaque greyish-green, up to 12cm/5in long, and ridged on the upper surface. They become a deep plum colour in autumn.

BUDS, FLOWERS AND FRUIT Flowers are borne in showy umbels followed by berries which change from green through scarlet to jet black and have a heavy, sour odour. The loosely domed clusters of five-petalled, creamy-white flowers are up to 10cm/4in across, appearing at the tips of branches in May and June, followed by clusters of shiny, slightly flattened, oval berries from July to September.

PLANT–ANIMAL RELATIONSHIPS The wayfaring-tree, like so many native trees and shrubs, is good for wildlife as it is host to many insect species, which in turn are consumed by birds and other animals. Its flowers burst into bloom early and their nectar at the base and pollen are an early source of nourishment for pollinating hoverflies and other insects. The berries, although unpalatable to humans, are eaten by birds in winter. The caterpillars of a species of tortricoid moth eat the leaves from June to August.

HISTORICAL AND OTHER USES Among the varied uses of the colours extracted from the ripe berries were black hair dye and ink. In Germany the young pliant stems joined willow and reeds to be made into baskets. The wood withstands the crushing of teeth so was used to make mouthpieces for tobacco-pipes.

NAME *Viburnum* supposedly from Latin *vies*, tie or bind, because young branches were used for tying. The common name was given by Gerard and, according to Geoffrey Grigson, is due to a mistranslation: he took the French name *viorne* to mean something ornamenting the road, the shrub 'seen by wayfarers'.

Viburnum opulus (Caprifoliaceae)

GUELDER ROSE

Here's the spring back or close,
When the almond-blossom blows:
We shall have the word
In a minor third
There is none but the cuckoo knows:
Heaps of the guelder-rose!
I must bear with it, I suppose
  'A Lover's Quarrel', Robert Browning (1812–89)

The lovely lace-like summer flowers followed by brilliant scarlet fruit and tinted foliage are among the beauties of this vigorous deciduous shrub. Not a rose, but a member of the genus *Viburnum*, it is a superb shrub, providing beauty in return for little effort. Suitable for borders, woodland corners, damp hollows, river banks, underwoods, hedges or simply as a stand-alone shrub, it grows in sun or semi-shade, but requires sun to flower and fruit well. Thriving on most moist but well-drained soils, except the most acid, it also tolerates drier, sandy garden soils and regenerates well after cutting when trimmed into shape. As it is liable to send out suckers from the roots, it colonises open ground if given the chance. William Robinson encouraged gardeners to grow it, bemoaning the fact that native viburnums were not well known and stressing that 'few shrubs of any countries are so handsome in blossom and berry as the Water Elder (*V. opulus*) . . . We search the world over for flowering shrubs – not one of which is prettier than the Water Elder, common in Sussex woods, and often seen near the water-side in Surrey.'

GROWTH HABIT Rarely more than 4m/13ft, usually half that height, it is spreading and bushy in habit.

PROPAGATION The method of propagation is the same as for the wayfaring-tree, but it does not germinate as readily.

ROLE IN LANDSCAPE It is found on moist, moderately acid or alkaline soils throughout Britain, but has become a scarce shrub of most woodland margins, hedgerows, scrub and marshes.

TRUNK AND BARK Its thicket-forming stems are erect, grey and smooth, with slightly angular, greenish twigs and branches that later become reddish-brown.

LEAVES The opposite pairs of young, maple-like leaves soon shed their downy covering, expanding up to 8cm/3in across with three to five irregularly toothed lobes. The leaves turn to shades of russet and orange or yellow and rich crimson before falling in late autumn.

BUDS, FLOWERS AND FRUIT In June and July the curious, flat-topped clusters of white flowers appear at the tips of branches. Unlike honeysuckle which is so strongly scented after dusk, the flowers of the guelder rose have no perfume. The outer, creamy-white flowers of each cluster are sterile; only the small inner flowers later produce the pretty glistening pink and white berries. By September and October these turn into one-seeded, translucent red berries; sometimes the bush appears to drip with their loose, hanging clusters. These may remain until leaf-fall.

PLANT–ANIMAL RELATIONSHIPS Guelder rose is an important resource for wildlife, providing food for 150 insect species, including beetles, bees, hoverflies, leaf-hoppers and sawflies, and 70 species of moth, including gold tail and mottled umber. The crimson berries, though slightly poisonous to man, are a seasonal winter feast for small mammals and birds including blackbirds, fieldfares and redwings. The dense tangles make good nesting sites.

HISTORICAL AND OTHER USES The young shoots were sometimes used for the tubes of tobacco pipes.

NAME The name given by Gerard in 1597, 'Gelders Rose', was due to its likeness to the cultivated garden snowball tree (*Geldersche roos*), from the province of Guelderland, Holland, which has sterile but showy blossoms.

Plate 78   78

capsule red brown outside
whitish inside with fine
silky ~~hoops~~ pappus.

young stem green old aspen

Salix herbacea

Near Caendochan, Augus. 3000 ft.
June 16. 1931.   Wm.

that Corrie of Clova 2600 ft.
Aug 7. 1929.

GETTING NEW PLANTS IN THE GROUND

It is better to plant trees and shrubs when they are young and small so that the roots have a chance to anchor themselves. Deciduous trees should be moved when dormant, before the spring when they will be in vigorous growth. Unless the tree is container-grown, planting is usually carried out during the dormant period between autumn and spring when the ground is warm. Nursery-grown shrubs and trees in pots or bags are not usually affected by transplanting if care is taken not to interfere with the root system.

When buying a plant in a container, check that the roots are not too matted or pot bound, although they can be spread out at the time of transplanting. Dig a hole about 1½ times the size of the rootball; line the hole with a mix of good garden soil and compost which, as well as breaking down, retains moisture; drive in a stake about 2m/7ft long; form a hill of soil in the hole and spread the roots loosely over the hill; add more soil and compost mixture, rotted farm manure or leaf mould. Finally, tramp in when about half full and fill until a little above the old soil line, watering in well and mulching the top. Stake with flexible ties and, if necessary, protect against rabbits and other animals.

In Britain where most of the rain is gentle, it is best if the soil forms a shallow basin around the stem, so moisture will drain in towards the stem and then down to the roots. But where there is heavy rainfall, for example in the west country or Ireland, the soil should be flat. Some gardeners fill holes with water first but this is inadvisable where there is loam or clay: surplus water encourages the soil to cake and pack densely so it sets hard when dry, which impedes growth. Water will also not drain away easily on clay, and will deprive the roots of oxygen.

PROPAGATION

To obtain good, sturdy and healthy plants, propagation is best effected by seed. Seeds are just embryo plants packaged with a stored food supply until conditions are right for germination – a protection for the winter when they remain dormant. As Professor Salisbury has written: 'Thought of from the plant's standpoint, the seed may be regarded as a device by which the offspring is protected, either whilst it is carried away from the parent or during unfavourable conditions.'

A plant grown from cuttings, on the other hand, is like a clone – an extension of the existing tree, not a new individual with two parents. It has the same strong points and defects, and is susceptible to the same diseases and problems, as it lacks the genetic variation achieved by sexual reproduction. A survey by the Wildlife Trusts revealed that most examples of black poplar in Britain were propagated from cuttings from around six hundred parent plants, a situation exacerbated by more male than female trees being planted (females were thought to be a nuisance due to the drifting white down from their catkins).

In contrast, reproduction by seed is the result of cross-pollination by insects, other animals or the wind, and requires separate flowers, one male and one female. Plants conceived in this way result in individuals with their own characteristics. Trees grown from seed have increased resistance to epidemics, diseases and pests. They ensure the survival of local genetic strains which would otherwise be swamped by trees of non-local or even non-British origin.

While most plants require pollination, this does not always lead to fertilisation – occasionally the egg grows into an embryo without being fertilised. This can happen with species of *Crataegus*, *Rubus* and *Taraxacum*, which sometimes produce direct clones.

ASEXUAL REPRODUCTION: SUCKERS AND SHOOTS

Sometimes, stems branch in all directions in an effort to reproduce by forming suckers. The vigorous shoots (rhizomes) go underground; the runners go on top of the ground. This method allows a single tree (such as ash or maple) or a herbaceous plant (such as strawberry) to make the most of a favourable habitat by producing identical daughter plants. It is a way of overcoming overcrowding and competition, but the result is the production of clones.

ASEXUAL REPRODUCTION: CUTTINGS

Softwood cuttings, pieces taken from newly formed shoots, need to be kept in a frame or hothouse until they have formed roots. Hardwood cuttings, usually taken from the growth of the previous season, can often be rooted in the open. If cuttings are taken with a 'heel', usually from the base or other growing point of the parent plant, these can sometimes, but not always, be damaging to the parent plant. 'Heel' cuttings contain auxin, a good growth-promoting hormone.

PROPAGATION CONTAINERS

Today, a wide variety of propagation vessels are used, ranging from inexpensive plastic trays and polystyrene blocks to shallow wooden trays. Some gardeners continue to use discarded plastic-coated cardboard cartons (cut down if too big), even yoghurt containers. These are ideal once drainage holes have been made in the bottom; small cuts at the side extending into the base enables drainage to continue if the container is placed on a flat surface. Fill it with sharp sand, with an alternative to sphagnum moss on the top, and sow the seed near the surface – if buried too deeply it may not germinate. To prevent drying out, the top of the container needs to be covered until green shoots are seen (most seeds do not need light to germinate – if they did, they would not come up when buried in the ground). When the new seedling has developed a few leaves, then put the plant in the ground. If using a milk carton, cut the bottom out and put both box and plant in the ground – milk cartons are robust and the sides will act as protective barriers against dehydration and competition from weeds.

STRATIFICATION AND SCARIFICATION

Many berries, including those of hawthorn, holly, wild roses and rowan, should be buried in sand-filled pots for a few months before sowing, unless they are stratified. Stratification is a temperature treatment used to break the seed's dormancy. Scarification, by contrast, is the deliberate wounding of the seed coat to allow water to enter. These processes are employed by modern gardeners to speed up germination when it is slow because of seed-coats that are impermeable to water, air or both. One way of removing the seed-coat from such seeds is by rubbing the coat with sandpaper. Other methods include immersion in special solutions, or even boiling water. As many seeds germinate more quickly after a particularly cold winter, some are put in refrigerators. More detailed information on these processes can be found in specialist books.

HOW HAS YOUR PLANT BEEN REPRODUCED?

No legislation stipulates that the method of reproduction, asexual or sexual, should be specified on labels in garden centres, but some nurseries now list origins in their catalogues. Many suppliers have a policy of increasing the use of seed from British seed sources. Some nurseries may, on request and for a fee, raise a plant from seed supplied by the customer if it is of acceptable origin.

This book recommends that plants should be raised from seeds.

LEAVES, COMPOST AND EARTHWORMS

THE IMPORTANCE OF LEAVES – DEAD AND ALIVE

Whether in containers, or in open heaps, the leaves of local native plants decompose better and more quickly than most exotics. As well as being environmentally friendly if they are left where they fall or in a compost heap, they can be virtual cafés for bats, birds, hedgehogs and other wildlife. When they are used as mulch they not only add a protective layer between the heat of the sun and the roots of the plant, but also give nutrients and help retain moisture and so save on water.

Different leaves result in different nutrient values and sustain different invertebrates. While the leaves of local species of oak, silver or downy birch, privet, bird cherry, beech and hazel disintegrate relatively quickly, holly leaves, due to their thickness, take much longer – and those of introduced species, such as the leaves of the London plane tree and eucalypts, are notoriously slow to decompose. Laurel and rhododendron actually produce dangerous gases when decomposing – if their leaves are squashed into a bin with a tight lid for a few weeks, make sure on opening it that you do not put your head too near the contents or you could pass out from the cyanide fumes.

For gardeners who find compost heaps complicated and dislike the heavy turning with spades and the procedures involved in getting the mixture right so that it heats up and breaks down quickly, leaves can be used in gardens in more simple ways:

- Leaves and twigs left in a pile produce mulch which, like other natural fertilisers, can be spread over flower beds each autumn to enrich and improve the soil.
- Collecting leaves and letting them slowly break down, releasing their nutrients back into the soil, is a natural process. Some can be spread immediately on garden beds; others can be left in a heap to rot down to form leaf mould – these do not need turning, nor do they depend on nitrogen-rich activators.
- If space allows, eco-heaps – piles of more bulky garden waste such as branches and garden debris – can be left to rot slowly over years.

These benefit the food chain, offer shelter for many creatures and are an easy solution to disposing of garden waste. They can be screened by trees or a hedge.

- Any pile of rotting leaves or compost provides sustenance for birds, butterflies and other wildlife. One cubic yard of beech wood litter contains large numbers of mites, springtails and numerous other invertebrates such as woodlice, millipedes, nematodes and round-worms. Insects feed on decaying leaves, helping to break them down into humus and plant nutrients. In turn these creatures provide food for higher animals, such as blackbirds, thrushes and hedgehogs.

The effect of mulch depends on the material used. For instance, pine needles can form a suffocating mat and their resin increases soil acidity. By contrast, the leaves of oak, beech, hazel and maple will act as a soft mulch as well as breaking down and adding organic matter to the soil as they are turned over by earthworms.

Artificial fertilisers have been widely available for only just over a century. Before that many things were used to enrich the soil of gardens: compost, manure, blood and bone, brewers' waste, seaweed, hoof and horn shavings from the blacksmith, cast-off clothes, old socks, rags, shoes, tins and imported coconut fibre.

COMPOST HEAPS

Compost-making is now treated as a science. Simple methods involve keeping it roughly in layers like the contents of a giant club sandwich, keeping it damp, balancing materials containing carbon and nitrogen, and building it on bare soil to encourage earthworms. It can be made in a square or a round bin and should be a minimum of about a square metre or yard to produce a high enough temperature. If it is just left in a pile it will lose too much heat to compost, but it will still, eventually, like all matter, break down.

Apart from air, heat and moisture, the secret of keeping the micro-organisms working lies in getting the proportions right between carbon and nitrogen (usually 25 parts carbon to 1 part nitrogen by weight). The amount of leaves put in the bin depends on whether they are native or introduced. Many gardeners prefer to have only 15–30 per cent of leaves forming part of any quickly decomposing compost, and make separate heaps for leaf mould.

It can be difficult to work out what the proportions are.

- Materials with high carbon values include dry leaves, sawdust, bark, straw, shredded newspaper, tissues, fireplace ash.
- Nitrogen is found in lawn clippings, vegetable and other kitchen scraps, the outer leaves of vegetables, cow, chicken or horse manure, coffee grounds.

Human urine is a good activator. Many a gardener makes discreet visits to the compost heap – another reason to have it hidden by a hedge.

To speed up decomposition, keep the heap covered with an old blanket, a sheet of polythene, a lid, hessian sacking or an old piece of carpet. Ensure that it never dries out by keeping it just damp; too much water will ruin it and make it smell and attract flies. Avoid introducing fat, oil, salt, disinfectants, pesticides or anything recently sprayed with insecticides – these all kill the vital bacteria, slowing down the process.

THE IMPORTANCE OF EARTHWORMS

Leaves not only help maintain the fertility of the soil but some, in turn, become meals for birds. Charles Darwin, the champion of recycling, wrote: 'Worms have played a more important part in the history of the world than most persons would suppose.' He likened their work to that of 'a gardener who prepares fine soil for his choicest plants'. Darwin spent 40 years investigating Britain's 24 species of earthworms (*Lumbricus*), calling them 'Nature's ploughshare'; he was the first to publicise the role they play in waste minimisation. In 1881, he published *The formation of vegetable moulds through the action of earthworms,* which showed how they enriched the soil by turning leaf litter into organic humus. He emphasised how earthworms consume, moisten and tear leaves to small shreds, partially digesting the vegetable matter and intimately mixing it with earth. His book forms the basis of much modern knowledge of soil fertility and structure, showing how worms convey decayed vegetation to their humus-lined burrow and eat it. Then they swallow earth, grind it to a powder and bring it to the surface, where it is discarded as worm castings. Thus earthworms move, till, aerate and enrich the earth.

To determine the rate at which objects sank into the ground, Darwin constructed a 'wormstone' on his own lawn, a flat rock to which he attached a measuring scale. He calculated that earthworms 'sank' the stone at the rate of 0.5cm/¼in a year, and horrified prudish Victorians by claiming that all the vegetable matter in England has, time and time again, passed through the intestinal tracts of earthworms.

While rehabilitating the character of earthworms, he tested leaves to see which ones tickled their palate. He also studied their habits, their anatomy, even their reaction to sound. When his son Frank played his bassoon they did not respond, but when they were placed on the piano and a bass note was struck, they were disturbed. Darwin reasoned that they were reacting to vibrations rather than sound. He also proved that they felt pain.

Many people do not distinguish between compost worms and earthworms. Every year, millions of worms are condemned to needless death through lack of knowledge. Compost worms – the sort that are sold for wormeries such as tiger worms – need a richer, damper, more humid environment than earthworms. In the wild, compost worms occupy the litter layer of forest and grasslands, eating dead leaves and animals and animal droppings; they like damp situations and rich worm food. Although some species burrow in the topsoil they do not penetrate far. Earthworms burrow at all levels of the topsoil – often as deep as a metre – and eat their way through the earth consuming organic matter such as decaying leaves, dead animals and dead roots. Some spend a lifetime underground, while others come nightly to the surface to gather leaves and other edibles. Gardeners can buy compost worms commercially, but they cannot buy earthworms. Alas, when people 'liberate' worms from their compost bins, they are unable to live in soil without rich, damp humus and they die.

Earthworms are also reliable indicators of pollution. If they stay away from any compost which has been kept moist and covered for some weeks, it may mean that the heap contains something toxic.

USING NATIVE TREES AND SHRUBS IN THE GARDEN

TREES FOR HERBACEOUS BORDERS

In many gardens, herbaceous borders also contain shrubs to add interest during the whole year. A herbaceous border could be based around guelder rose and coppiced hazel to give structure, particularly in autumn and winter. On lighter, more acidic soils, broom and heather can be substituted – as can dogwood in moister soils and daphne in basic soils, with bulbs beneath and herbs between. Taller teasle, ornamental thistles, willowherb, foxglove and campanula at the back can grade into mallow, columbine, goldenrod, campion, oxeye daisy, valerian and hemp agrimony. In the middle of the border use lords and ladies, ornamental thistles, spiked speedwell, Jacob's ladder, toadflax, scabious, avens; at the front, meadow cranesbill. Drifts of daffodills can be planted under deciduous shrubs; gaps can be filled with primrose, lily of the valley and field pansy. Hellebore and bold clumps of grass, chosen for a long season of flowering, also grow well near many trees.

CONTROLLING TREE SIZE IN GARDENS

Many gardeners are nervous of having large trees in gardens, but they need not be worried if they are kept small, as in hedges. Roots only grow because of the starch they receive from leaves, so if a tree is never allowed to gain much height it will never have a large root system (an extreme example of inhibiting roots is the Japanese practice of bonsai). In this way, with annual pruning, large trees can be safely grown in gardens. The late director of the Royal Botanic Gardens, Kew, Professor E. J. Salisbury, emphasised in his book *The Living Garden* that pruning and coppicing inhibits root growth. 'Experiments seem to indicate that repeated cutting of either grass or shrubs tends to check the root development. Hence, to diminish the competitive influence of shrubs for water as far as possible, it would appear that continuous trimming is more likely to be effective than if appreciable growth is permitted between the intervals of cutting. If vigorous shoot growth be permitted at any time unchecked, there will be corresponding development in the root system. When the shoots are subsequently cut back the plant will have an extent of root larger in proportion to the size of the shoot system, and the latter will, therefore, tend to grow more rapidly than if it had been constantly kept in check. The converse is also true, and sometimes a hedge which lacks vigour can be encouraged in its growth by deliberately permitting a longer period of growth before cutting back . . . the more even the trimming the more completely will the shoots and leaves of the plant afford protection to one another from the drying action of the wind, so that a badly trimmed hedge probably makes appreciably greater demands upon the water-supply of the soil than one which is kept cut.'

The continual cutting of a hedge, as with a lawn, is also a constant drain on the soil, so hedges need more compost than trees.

HEDGES AND HEDGEROWS

Hedgerows have been part of the landscape of the British Isles since Neolithic man started to clear the forests 6,000 years ago. But changes in farming and the expansion of towns since the Second World War have meant that 200,000 miles of farm hedges have been wiped out in England alone. To re-create hedgerows, British Trees & Shrubs, near Bath, provides five plants per metre for double-line planting of a thick 'stock-proof' hedge, using the following proportions:

- 60 per cent hawthorn
- 15 per cent hazel
- 5 per cent each blackthorn, field maple, dogwood
- 4 per cent crab apple
- 2 per cent each spindle, holly, dog rose

More formal hedges were first grown in Britain by the Romans during their occupation between 47BC and AD270. They introduced new species, including the walnut and cultivated roses, laurel and Norway spruce, but used local species of yew and box for hedges. The layout of early Romano-British gardens was confirmed during excavations by archaeologists at the Roman Palace and Museum at Fishbourne, on the coast of Sussex, where the ancient garden has been re-created.

NATIVE TREES FOR PLANTING IN HEDGES

Beech	Elder	Ivy
Blackberry	Field maple	Oak
Blackthorn	Hawthorn	Old man's beard
Box	Hazel	Spindle
Crab apple	Holly	Yew
Dog rose	Honeysuckle	
Dogwood	Hornbeam	

As well as adding strong design to a garden, hedges are multi-purpose, giving shelter and privacy while creating a habitat for birds and other animals. Their numbers have increased with new fashions: turning gardens into a series of different areas or 'rooms', and using straight lines to give a sense of order in contrast to a profusion of annual or perennial flowers. William Morris urged gardeners to use hedges or fences and 'then to fill up the flower-growing space with things that are free and interesting in their growth, leaving Nature to do the desired complexity, which she will certainly not fail to do'. At Hidcote Manor, Gloucestershire, among the inspiring examples of clipped hedges is a spectacular display of yew, box, holly, beech and hornbeam, emphasising the differing leaf textures and shades of green.

Hedges provide both food and safe nesting sites for birds which search for berries and insects. Monocultural hedges – just a single species such as privet, yew or box – are not as hospitable as a mixed hedge which will have different plants coming into leaf, flower and fruit at different times.

TREES BY SIZE

LARGE (30 METRES / 100 FEET AND HIGHER)

Carpinus betula	Hornbeam
Fagus sylvatica	Beech
Fraxinus excelsio	Ash
Pinus sylvestris	Scots pine
Populus nigra	Black poplar
Quercus petraea	Sessile oak
Quercus robur	Pedunculate oak
Tilia cordata	Small-leaved lime
Ulmus glabra	Wych elm

MEDIUM (15–30 METRES / 50–100 FEET)

Acer campestre	Field maple
Alnus glutinosa	Alder
Betula pendula	Silver birch
Betula pubescens	Downy birch
Populus tremula	Aspen
Salix fragilis	Crack willow
Salix pentandra	Bay willow
Sorbus aria	Whitebeam
Sorbus aucuparia	Rowan
Sorbus torminalis	Wild service-tree
Taxus baccata	Yew

SMALL (15 METRES / 50 FEET AND LOWER)

Arbutus unedo	Strawberry tree
Buxus sempervirens	Box
Corylus avellana	Hazel
Crataegus laevigata	Midland hawthorn
Crataegus monogyna	Hawthorn
Ilex aquifolium	Holly
Juniperus communis	Juniper
Malus sylvestris	Crab apple
Prunus avium	Wild cherry
Prunus padus	Bird cherry
Salix alba	White willow
Salix caprea	Goat willow

RHS LIST OF BRITISH NATIVE TREES AND LARGER SHRUBS

The Royal Horticultural Society's list includes any species or hybrid growing to 5m/16½ft or more in height, which is thus deemed capable of being trained as a tree under garden conditions. The result was 86 trees and larger shrubs. Those followed by • have full entries in this book.

Acer campestre •
Alnus glutinosa •
Arbutus unedo •
   (native in Ireland)
Betula × *aurata*
Betula × *intermedia*
   (some forms*)*
Betula pendula •
Betula pubescens
Buxus sempervirens •
Carpinus betulus •
Corylus avellana •
Crataegus laevigata
Crataegus × *media*
Crataegus monogyna •
Fagus sylvatica •
Frangula alnus •
Fraxinus excelsior •
Hippophae rhamnoides •
Ilex aquifolium •
Juniperus communis •
Malus sylvestris •
Pinus sylvestris •
Populus × *canescens*
Populus nigra •
Populus tremula •
Prunus avium •
Prunus padus •
Prunus spinosa •
Pyrus cordata
Quercus petraea
Quercus robur •

Quercus × *rosacea*
Rhamnus cathartica •
Salix alba •
Salix × *alopecuroides*
Salix × *calodendron*
Salix caprea •
Salix × *capreola*
Salix cinerea •
Salix fragilis
Salix × *fruticosa*
Salix × *latifolia*
Salix × *lintonii*
Salix × *meyeriana*
Salix × *mollisima*
Salix × *multinervis*
Salix pentandra
Salix × *pontederiana*
Salix purpurea
Salix × *reichardtii*
Salix × *rubens*
Salix × *rubra*
Salix × *sericans*
Salix × *smithiana*
Salix × *stipularis*
Salix triandra
Salix viminalis
Sambucus nigra •
Sorbus aria •
Sorbus arranensis
Sorbus aucuparia •
Sorbus bristoliensis
Sorbus devoniensis

Sorbus domestica
Sorbus eminens
Sorbus hibernica
Sorbus lancastriensis
Sorbus porrigentiformis
Sorbus pseudofennica
Sorbus rupicola
Sorbus subcuneata
Sorbus torminalis •
Sorbus × *vagensis*
Sorbus vexans
Sorbus wilmottiana
Taxus baccata •
Tilia × *europaea*
Tilia cordata •
Tilia platyphyllos
Ulmus × *elegantissima*
Ulmus glabra •
Ulmus × *hollandica*
Ulmus minor
Ulmus plotii
Ulmus procera •
Ulmus × *vegeta*
Ulmus × *viminalis*

TREES FOR SPECIAL REQUIREMENTS

FAST-GROWING SOFTWOOD (FOR DAMP SITES)

Alnus glutinosa	Alder
Tilia cordata	Small-leaved lime
Populus nigra	Black poplar
Salix	Willow, all species

BROAD-LEAVED

Fraxinus excelsior	Ash
Fagus sylvatica	Beech
Betula pendula	Silver birch
Ulmus procera	Elm
Carpinus betulus	Hornbeam
Corylus avellana	Hazel
Quercus robur	Pedunculate oak

POLLUTION-RESISTANT

Fraxinus excelsior	Ash
Betula pendula	Silver birch
Malus sylvestris subsp *sylvestris*	Crab apple
Ilex aquifolium	Holly
Tilia cordata	Small-leaved lime
Ligustrum vulgare	Privet
Sorbus aucuparia	Rowan, mountain ash
Pinus sylvestris	Scots pine
Salix	Willow, all species
Sorbus aria	Common whitebeam
Taxus baccata	Yew

EVERGREENS

These are conifers with needles such as yew, and leathery-leaved types such as holly and box

Arbutus unedo	Strawberry tree
Buxus sempervirens	Box
Calluna vulgaris	Heather
Daphne laureola	Spurge laurel
Erica cinerea	Bell heather

Hedera helix   Ivy
Ilex aquifolium   Holly
Juniperus communis   Juniper
Myrica gale   Bog myrtle, sweet gale
Pinus sylvestris   Scots pine
Ruscus aculeatus   Butcher's broom
Taxus baccata   Yew
Ulex europaeus   Gorse
Ulex gallii   Western gorse
Ulex minor   Dwarf gorse
Vaccinium oxycoccos   Cranberry
Vaccinium vitis-idea   Cowberry

SPECTACULAR RED BERRIES
Arbutus unedo   Strawberry tree
Berberis vulgaris   Wild barberry
Crataegus laevigata   Midland hawthorn
Crataegus monogyna   Hawthorn
Daphne mezereum   Mezereon (daphne)
Ilex aquifolium   Holly
Prunus avium   Wild cherry, gean
Ruscus aculeatus   Butcher's broom
Solanum dulcamara   Woody nightshade, bittersweet
Sorbus aucuparia   Rowan, mountain ash
Vaccinium oxycoccos   Cranberry
Viburnum opulus   Guelder rose

CLIMBERS
Clematis vitalba   Travellers' joy, old man's beard
Hedera helix   Ivy
Humulus lupulus   Hop
Lonicera periclymenum   Honeysuckle
Ribes nigrum   Blackcurrant
Ribes rubrum   Redcurrant
Ribes uva-crispa   Gooseberry
Rosa arvensis   Field rose
Rosa canina   Dog-rose
Rosa pimpinellifolia   Burnet rose

BRITISH NATIVE TREES AND POSSIBLE HOUSE DAMAGE

Sort of tree		Normal mature height in clay soils in urban setting (m)	Problems may occur with shallow foundations if planted closer than these distances (m) on shrinkable clay soils
Ash	Fraxinus	23	10
Beech	Fagus	20	9
Birch	Betula	12–14	4–5
Hawthorn	Crataegus	10	5–7
Holly	Ilex	12–14	3
Lime	Tilia	18–24	8–11
Oak	Quercus	16–23	18
Pine	Pinus	20–29	8
Whitebeam, Rowan	Sorbus	8–12	5-7
Willow	Salix	15–24	18
Yew	Taxus	8–12	5

This useful reference for anyone wanting to plant trees close to a house has been supplied by Professor David Cutler, Royal Botanic Gardens, Kew.

Notes relating to trees recorded in Kew survey
This is some of the information gathered by the Kew Tree Root Survey. The records relate to trees which were thought to be connected with damage to buildings; they are historical and should not be used predictively. There could be problems with occasional trees planted further away than indicated.

roots often very shallow; crown tolerant of pruning
rarely implicated in damage; scarce on clay; old trees may become unstable because of root rot, but unsuitable for small gardens
* low implication in damage; older trees tolerate only light pruning
* soil close to hedges may dry excessively; tolerates heavy pruning
* rarely implicated in damage; tolerates heavy pruning
manageable at closer distances, tolerates heavy pruning, but best avoided in small gardens
one of the more problematic genera; avoid
rarely implicated in damage, but can be too large for a small or medium-sized garden
* relatively unproblematic; tolerates heavy pruning
one of the more problematic genera; tolerates heavy pruning; avoid
* rarely implicated in damage; can be pruned hard

Those marked * pose least problems. Roots of most of these will penetrate cracked or seeping drains; intact drains are thought to be safe from root invasion. Buildings on soils that do not shrink on drying are generally considered to be little affected by tree roots. Most native shrubs have appeared very infrequently in cases of foundation damage, but thick planting within 2–3m/7–10ft of shallowly founded buildings on shrinkable clay soils should be avoided.

SUPPLIERS

NATIVE TREES

The Forestry Commission
www.forestry.gov.uk

The Native Tree Shop Support Service team
The Woodland Trust, Autumn Court
Grantham, Lincolnshire NG31 6LL
Tel.: 01476 581111
nativetreeshop@woodland-trust.org

Horticultural Trades Association, Forestry Nursery Group
www.the-hta.org

For a complete list of suppliers of native trees and shrubs visit
Flora Locale
www.floralocale.org

SUPPLIERS AND GROWERS

FREE TREES from the Countryside Stewardship Scheme
Applicable in certain rural areas
Details from DEFRA
Tel. : 020 7238 6000
www.defra.gov.uk/erdp/schemes/css/default.htm

Alba Trees plc
Lower Winton
Gladsmuir, East Lothian EH33 2AL
Tel.: 01620 825058
www.alba-trees.co.uk
sales@alba-trees.co.uk

British Trees & Shrubs
125 Hansford Square
Combe Down
Bath, Somerset BA2 5LL
Tel.: 01225 840080
Mail order

British Wildflower Plants
31 Main Road
North Burlingham, Norfolk NR13 4TA
Tel.: 01603 716615
www.wildflowers.co.uk
linda@wildflowers.co.uk
Mail order

BTCV Enterprises Ltd
The Conservation Centre
163 Balby Road
Balby, Doncaster DN4 0RH
Tel.: 01302 572244
www.btcv.org

Chew Valley Trees
Winford Road
Bristol BS40 8QE
Tel.: 01275 333 752
www.chewvalleytreesandlandscapes.co.uk
info@chewvalleytrees.co.uk

Firecrest Nurseries
Hall Road
Little Bealings
Woodbridge, Suffolk IP13 6LU
Tel./fax 01473 625937
www.firecrest.org.uk

The London Wildlife Trust Garden Centre
28 Marsden Road
London SE15 4EE
Tel.: 020 7252 9186
www.wildlifetrust.org.uk/london
lwtwildgarden@cix.co.uk

Maelor Nurseries Ltd
Fields Farm , Bronington
Whitchurch, Shropshire SY13 3HZ
Tel.: 01948 710606
www.maelor.co.uk
sales@maelor.co.uk

Trees Please
Low Urpeth Farm, Ouston
Chester-le-Street, Durham DH2 1BD
Tel.: 01914 103233
treesplease@btinternet.com

Woodland Improvement and Conservation Ltd
Newent Lane
Huntley, Gloucestershire GL19 3HG
Tel.: 01452 830344
www.tree-shop.co.uk
Offers traceable native trees

COMPOST

Original Organics Ltd
  Unit 9, Langlands Business Park
  Uffculme, Devon EX15 3DA
  Tel.: 01884 841515
  www.originalorganics.co.uk
  sales@originalorganics.co.uk
  Plastic bins and wormeries

Archwood Greenhouses
  Robinwood
  Goodrich, Herefordshire HR9 6HT
  Tel.: 01600 890125
  www.archwoodgreenhouses.com
  info@archwood.wanadoo.co.uk
  Slatted wooden bins

LEAFLETS AND BOOKS ABOUT ORGANIC GARDENING

Henry Doubleday Research Association
  Ryton Organic Gardens
  Ryton-on-Dunsmore
  Coventry, West Midlands CV8 3LG
  Tel.: 024 7630 3517
  www.hdra.org.uk
  enquiry@hdra.org.uk

HELPFUL PUBLICATIONS

Allison, Keith, *A Guide to Plants Poisonous to Horses*, J. A. Allen, London 1997

Bean, W. J., *Trees and Shrubs Hardy in the British Isles*, 1914; 1933

Beckett, Kenneth and Gillian, *Planting Native Trees and Shrubs*, Jarrold, Norwich 1979

Chinery, Michael, *The Living Garden*, Dorling Kindersley, London 1971

Chinery, Michael, *The Natural History of the Garden*, Collins, London 1977

Chittenden, F. J., *Dictionary of Gardening*, OUP, Oxford 1956

Clapham, Tootin and Warburg, *Flora of the British Isles*, CUP, Cambridge 1962

Coats, Alice M., *Garden Shrubs and their Histories*, Vista Books, London 1963

Cobbett, William, *The English Gardener*, 1833

Culpeper, Nicholas, *The Complete Herbal and English Physician Enlarged*, 1653

Edlin, H. L., *British Woodland Trees*, Batsford, London 1944

Evelyn, John, *Sylva, or A Discourse on Forest-Trees*, 1664

Flora Facts & Fables, ed. Grace Corne, Norfolk, quarterly since 1994

Gerard, John, *The Herball, or Historie of Plants*, 1597

Gerard, John, ed. Johnson, *The Herball, or Generall Historie of Plantes*, 1633

Godwin, H., *History of the British Flora*, 1956

Grieve, Mrs M., *A Modern Herbal*, 1931; available as hyper-text at http://botanical.com/botanical/mgmh/mgmh.html

Hadfield, M., *Gardening in Britain*, 1961

Hamilton, Jill, Duchess of, Penny Hart and John Simmons, *The Gardens of William Morris*, Frances Lincoln, London 1998

Hamilton, Jill, Duchess of, Penny Hart and John Simmons, *English Plants for Your Garden*, Frances Lincoln, London 2000

Hamilton, Jill, Duchess of, and Dr Franklyn Perring, *Scottish Plants for Scottish Gardens*, Mercat Press, 3rd edition, 2000

Hemphill, John and Rosemary, *The Fragrant Garden*, Collins/ Angus & Robertson, Sydney 1992

Hibberd, S., *The Ivy*, 1872

Hobhouse, Penelope, *A Book of Gardening*, National Trust, London 1987

Humphries, C. J., J. R. Press and D. Sutton, *The Hamlyn Guide to Trees of Britain and Europe*, Hamlyn, London 1981

Huxley, A., *The New RHS Dictionary of Gardening*, Macmillan, London 1992

Keble Martin, W., *The New Concise Flora in Colour*, Ebury Press & Michael Joseph, London 1965

Kerr, Jessica, *Shakespeare's Flowers*, Kestrel Books, London 1969

Meikle, D., *Willows and Poplars of Great Britain and Ireland*, BSBI, London 1984

Miller, Philip, *The Gardener's Dictionary*, 7th edn. 1759

Miller, Philip, ed. Martyn, *The Gardener's Dictionary*, 9th edn. 1805

Parkinson, John, *Paradisi in Sole, Paradisus Terrestris*, 1629

Parkinson, John, *Theatrum Botanicum*, 1640

Polunin, Oleg, *Flowers of Europe*, OUP, Oxford 1969

Pratt, Anne, *Flowering Plants of Great Britain*, 1855

Ray, John, *Catalogus Plantarum Angliae*, 1677

Reader's Digest Field Guide to the Trees and Shrubs of Britain, ed. Michael W. Davison, Reader's Digest Association, London 1981

Robinson, William, *The Wild Garden*, reprinted from the original 1894 edition by The Scholar Press, Yorkshire 1977

Salisbury, E. J., *The Living Garden*, G. Bell, London 1942

Schwankl, A., *What Wood is That?* Thames & Hudson, London 1956

Stace, Clive, *New Flora of the British Isles*, CUP, Cambridge 1991

Taylor, David and Yvonne, *The Compost Book*, Reed, New Holland, Sydney 1993; 1998

Taylor, Jane, *Creative Planting with Climbers*, Ward Lock, London 1991

Thacker, Christopher, *The History of Gardens*, Croom Helm, Kent 1979

Vickery, Roy, *A Dictionary of Plant Lore*, Oxford 1995

PICTURE CREDITS

From W. H. Fitch with W. G. Smith, *Illustrations of the British Flora: a series of wood engravings, with dissections, of British Plants*, 4th revised edition, Lovell Reeve & Co., London 1919. The illustrations were reprinted from George Bentham, *Handbook of the British Flora: a description of the flowering plants and ferns indigenous to, or naturalised in the British Isles. Based on original drawings by W. Fitch*, Lovell Reeve & Co., London 1865
  pages 34, 35, 44, 57, 64, 70, 71, 79, 85, 88, 90, 93, 95, 97, 99, 103, 105, 111, 115, 123, 126, 129, 131, 139, 144, 157, 159, 164, 169, 171, 177, 181, 187, 194, 197, 201

From the Rev. C. A. Johns, *The Forest Trees of Britain*, Society for Promoting Christian Knowledge, London 1869
  pages 23, 26, 59, 121, 167, 190, 199

© The Estate of the Rev. William Keble Martin
  pages 2, 6, 8, 18, 28, 32, 37, 50, 53, 61, 67, 73, 106, 108, 117, 134, 137, 153, 154, 163, 165, 172, 174, 179, 184, 188, 193, 203, 207, 210

From John Claudius Loudon, *Arboretum et fruticetum Britannicum*, 8 volumes, Longman, London 1844
  pages 75, 77, 81, 83, 101, 125, 141, 147, 173

Created for Flora for Fauna by Barry Tobin
  pages 40, 66, 116, 119, 196, 205
  Back cover, L to R, top row: ash, silver birch, alder, wild cherry, hornbeam. Bottom row: mountain ash, small-leaved lime, hawthorn, field maple, hazel. Spine: beech leaf
  These can also be seen at www.floraoffulham.org

© Steven Wooster
  Front cover: oak

Distribution maps of the trees in this book can be seen at www.floraoffulham.org and at www.chrishumphries.com

INDEX BY COMMON NAME